MW01088166

An Amateur Botanist's
Identification Manual for the

Shrubs and Trees
of the Southern California Deserts

by

Jim W. Dole, Ph.D.
Department of Biology,
California State University
Northridge, California

and

Betty B. Rose, M.S.
Department of Biology
College of the Canyons
Valencia, California

Illustrated by:
Marianne D. Wallace, Marguerite Hammerly,
Paul L. Brookman, Jr., Jan Cordes, Phyllis Pearlman,
Kenneth Jones, Jr., and Jim W. Dole

Maps by:
Randal S. Thomson

© Copyright 1996
by Jim W. Dole and Betty B. Rose

Foot-loose Press
15857 Vincennes Street
North Hills, California 91343 USA
818-894-3640

All rights reserved. No part of this book may be
reproduced in any form without permission in writing from
the authors, except by a reviewer who may quote brief
passages in a review to be printed in a magazine or
newspaper.

This book is dedicated to:
Deborah, Phillip and **Robert,**
and to **Loren** and **Aaron.**

Preface

This book is an outgrowth of 25 years of teaching a class entitled "Plants and animals of southern California" at California State University, Northridge. Although the course was initiated by one of us (JWD), both of us have, at various times, been involved in its instruction.

Because the course is designed for "general education," students who enroll come from a variety of disciplines: recreation, geography, anthropology, even psychology, history, and business. Beyond a year of general biology, the students have little biological training. What most do have, however, is a keen interest in the natural environment, usually the result of earlier experiences during leisure activities such as camping, hiking and backpacking.

We have found our students eager to know more about the native organisms, the ones they encounter whenever they venture beyond the confines of the city. The first question they generally ask is: "What is it?" That is, they want a name they can attach to it, the first step in developing familiarity. Beyond that, however, we have discovered our students have a multitude of other questions. They want to know what the organisms does, how it affects them, if and how it was used by native Americans, how it influences other organisms, even how it is peculiarly adapted to survive where it does.

For the botanical portion of the class, we have found the standard guides to the southern California flora, books such as Hickman's *The Jepson Manual: Higher Plants of California* and Munz' *Flora of Southern California*, simply unusable. Effective use of such references requires a much more sophisticated knowledge of plants than our students have or have the time or interest to develop. Moreover, beyond identifying a plant, such books usually fail to provide answers to our students' many other questions. We have also found the many field guides to the flora of southern California unsuitable. Though many are technically excellent and beautifully illustrated, most are of limited use to persons not already acquainted with the flora. Beyond picture browsing, most provide no means whereby a reader can identify an unfamiliar plant with certainty. And they, like the larger botanical guides, typically contain little information about a plant beyond a brief description.

We wrote this book, then, to provide a means for persons with no technical botanical training to, with reasonable certainty, attach a name to a previously unfamiliar plant. To accomplish this, we have developed simplified keys that lead the reader step by step to the identity of the plant at hand. In the keys, we have avoided, insofar as possible, the jargon that besets so many botanical references. Moreover, we have constructed the keys so that identification is possible even when certain errors are made. For example, because our students commonly mistake the showy yellow sepals of Flannel bush for petals, we have included the plant in Key C - 5.2 (Flowers with separate petals), even though its flowers are apetalous.

In addition to the keys, we provide for each plant a synopsis of its characteristics, a map or description of its distribution, and a set of "general interest" notes. Descriptions, written in telegraphic style, provide sufficient information to verify a plant's identity; sketches of many species provide the reader a direct visual reference.

The focus of this book is the *common* trees and shrubs native to southern California, the ones that almost anyone who tramps the bush can expect to encounter eventually. Many rarer forms, less commonly encountered, have been omitted. In selecting a species for inclusion, we have allowed ourselves a degree of latitude to accommodate the interests and limitations of our students. For example, we have included some plants not normally considered shrubs or trees. Among these are the larger cacti, such non-woody plants as agaves, and a few shrubby plants that are merely woody at the base. We have also taken the liberty of including several non-native woody plants that have become naturalized in our area, recognizing that when encountering a plant growing away from human habitation, our students have no way of knowing which is and which is not a native.

We recognize that this book is far from perfect and are eager to improve it. We invite input as to changes that will make it better able to serve the audience for which it is intended. Whatever its limitations, we sincerely hope the book will not only enhance the enjoyment of its readers, but will increase their awareness of the importance and fragility of our natural vegetation. If it succeeds in this, our efforts will have been worthwhile.

Jim W. Dole
Betty B. Rose

Acknowledgments

We are extremely grateful to the many individuals who have had input in the preparation of this book.

We are especially grateful for the contributions of Marianne D. Wallace, the artist responsible for most of the illustrations in this book. Her skill in depicting each plant both accurately and artistically has both enhanced the appearance of the book and made it immensely more useful to the reader.

Many illustrations in this book were contributed by students — Marguerite Hammerly, Paul Brookman, Jr., Jan Cordes, Phyllis Pearlman — all of whom willingly spent their time sketching just for the experience. On several occasions, these amateur artists even accompanied us in our travels, sketching whenever the opportunity presented itself. Kenneth Jones, Jr. sketched the "fantasy flowers" that accompany the practice key. For the efforts and enthusiasm of all of these persons, we are exceedingly grateful.

Maps were prepared by Randal S. Thomson from information provided by the authors. We believe the maps add to the usefulness of the book and for his efforts we express our sincere thanks.

Dr. Gary Wallace, former Curator of Botany, Los Angeles County Museum of Natural History, read and provided helpful comments on portions of the manuscript; he also aided us in obtaining and identifying several plants. Dr. Kenneth Wilson, Professor of Biology and Director of the California State University, Northridge, Herbarium, allowed us access to many herbarium specimens. Joy Nishida, curator of the California State University, Northridge, Herbarium, aided us in identification on many occasions. Some herbarium specimens were provided by the Rancho Santa Anna Botanical Garden. To all we express our gratitude.

Last, but by no means least, we acknowledge the contributions of the hundreds of students who have passed through our courses. In truth, it is they — and their never-ending questions — that have provided the stimulation and the inspiration for this book. Without their constant queries, this book would never have been written.

J.W.D. and B.B.R.

Table of Contents

	Key to Fantasy Flowers
1	**A**—Plant multifaced . . . . .Go to 2
	B—Plant single-faced . . . Go to 3
2	**A**—Faces united by vines . . . . . .
	. . . . Cackling cacopholily
	B—Faces in a tight cluster . . . . . .
	. . . . Gregarious groupie
3	**A**—Plant with sharp spines . . . . .
	. . . . Prickly parry
	B—No spines present . . . Go to 4
4	**A**—Flowers happy faced . Go to 5
	B—Flowers with dour faces . . . . .
	. . . . Solitary longpuss
5	**A**—With long eyelashes . . . .
	. . . . Frilly fritellary
	B—Without long eyelashes. . . . . .
	. . . Knee-slapping nasturtium

How to Use This Book

This book is designed to allow any reasonably observant person, even one with no botanical training, to identify the major species of shrubs and trees that grow naturally in southern California. Several non-native species that have become naturalized — those sufficiently at home in our climate that they regularly propagate themselves without human intervention — are also included, for there is no way for a novice to tell a native from a naturalized species. However, the myriad ornamental plants that adorn our cities and the native herbaceous (non-woody) plants are beyond the scope of this book.

Identifying a Plant

Using a Dichotomous Key

The standard tool used by botanists to identify plants is the *dichotomous key*. Typically, such a device is composed of several pairs, or *couplets*, of contrasting characters. Beginning with the first couplet, the reader chooses the member, or *lead*, that best fits the organism at hand. The choice made, the reader is directed to a second couplet and from this to a third, and so on, until eventually arriving at the organism's name.

The key to the "fantasy flowers" on the facing page illustrates how the system works. Using it, we will "key out" one of the imaginary plants shown, say, the one in the upper left corner. Starting with the first couplet of the key, we note that the unknown plant best fits the second lead; that is, it has but one face. Having made that choice, we are directed to couplet 3. Skipping the second couplet, we find that couplet 3 offers a choice between plants with spines and those without. Since ours is spineless, we choose the second lead and are directed this time to couplet 4. Here, because our flower appears sad, we choose the second lead, "flowers with dour faces." This choice leads us to the discovery that our plant is a "Solitary Longpuss."

Using the Main Key

The main key of this book is constructed on the pattern of our fantasy key and is used similarly. However, because the number of choices in our key is large, the main key has been subdivided so that it consists of keys within keys. This means that occasionally you will be directed not to another couplet, but to another key. Moving to the new key and beginning with that key's first couplet, the process is repeated. Although not difficult to use, a note of caution is in order. You must remember to always move from couplet to couplet within a given key unless specifically directed to move to another key!

As you move through the main key, you will note that, in some cases, you are lead ultimately to a specific name of the plant. This is true, in general, when a plant has no (or few) close relatives in our area with which it might be confused. In others instances, the key terminates with the name of the group, what botanists call the *genus*, to which the plant belongs. To discover the specific name of the plant, that is, to determine its *species*, you must turn to still another key elsewhere in the book where more choices must be made.

Using Species Keys

Turning to the page indicated, you will find another key similar to those with which you are already familiar. Here you should continue the procedure already described until arriving at the plant's name.

Typically, the species keys also contain information about each plant's distribution. This information may prove useful in your final determination of a plant's identity, for it may permit the elimination of some possibilities because the plant in which you are interested is outside a species' known range. The distribution maps for some species may also be of help, but keep in mind that the boundaries indicated on the maps are not precise. Use this information with caution.

Checking Your Identification

Although using a key is simple, at least in principle, it is not foolproof. Mistakes are easily made, either because descriptions in the key are misinterpreted or because the specimen at hand is not "typical" of the species. Or, sometimes, the set of characters chosen for the key is not completely clear, as, for instance, a choice between "flowers yellow" or "flowers cream-colored to white." (We have tried our best to avoid this sort of ambiguity, but occasionally we were simply unable to do so.) Whatever the reason, the result of making a wrong choice in the key is misidentification of the plant.

All identifications based on the key are tentative and must be confirmed by checking the plant against the description of the species provided. To save space, all descriptions have been written in "telegraphic style;" only key descriptive words are included and many abbreviations are used. It is a good idea to familiarize yourself with the list of standard abbreviations in the appendix before attempting to verify a plant's identity for the first time.

Sketches, where provided, also are useful aids in confirming a plant's identity, as is the information provided about each plant's distribution within southern California. If you arrive at a tentative identification and your specimen looks quite unlike the sketch, or if you found your plant in, say, Los Angeles County but the key says the species grows only near San Diego, it is likely that you have made a wrong turn in the key. If so, you should "re-key" the plant, paying particular attention to those couplets where you were unsure on your first attempt.

Wherever it seemed likely that a rare species that was excluded from the key might be misidentified as a more common form, we have added a note to that effect. Under sandpaper plant, for instance, a note calls attention to similar-appearing but less common species that were not included in the key. By noting the rarer plants' key diagnostic characters and distribution, it should be possible to distinguish between them.

3

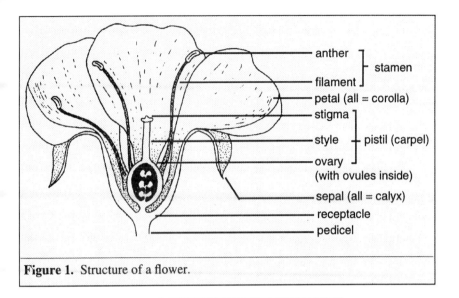

Figure 1. Structure of a flower.

Flowers and Inflorescences

To use the keys in this book, it is first necessary to become familiar with basic plant structure. It is especially important to know the parts of a plant's reproductive organs — its flowers or cones — for much botanical classification is based on their arrangement.

A "Standard" Flower

In its simplest form a flower consists of four sets of parts arranged in concentric rings, or whorls, on the expanded end of a flower stalk (figure 1). The flower stalk is called the **pedicel**, its expanded end, the **receptacle**.

Sepals, collectively termed the **calyx**, form the outermost ring of flower parts. Just within the calyx lie the **petals**; all the petals together comprise the **corolla**. The calyx and the corolla together are sometimes referred to as the **perianth**. The sepals enclose the petals and other parts of the flower when in bud, but with the flower's opening they are overshadowed by the petals. Petals are commonly brightly colored or white; some sepals are as colorful as petals, but most are green. The sepals and petals surround the reproductive organs but are not themselves directly involved in reproduction.

In the center of the flower is the female reproductive organ, the **pistil**. The expanded base of the pistil, the **ovary**, houses one or more seeds-to-be, called **ovules**, in a

4

chamber called a **locule** or **cell**. Extending from the ovary is a narrow necklike **style** capped by a **stigma**.

Surrounding the pistil are the male reproductive organs, the **stamens**. Each stamen consists of a narrow support structure, or **filament**, at the end of which is a saclike **anther**. The anthers produce **pollen**, the male reproductive cells. Some stamens lack anthers, hence are **sterile**.

Fusion of Flower Parts

Each of the parts of a flower is often separate and distinct, but this is not always the case. The edges of petals, for instance, may be united, sometimes only at the base, sometimes almost their entire length. Fusion of petals is not always obvious, especially if they are joined only at the base; if a petal can be removed easily without pulling others with it, the petals are probably separate. When petals are fused, the corolla may take the shape of a tube, a trumpet, a bell, an urn, even a saucer. Several common configurations of united petals are shown in figure 2. Sepals may be united in a similar manner.

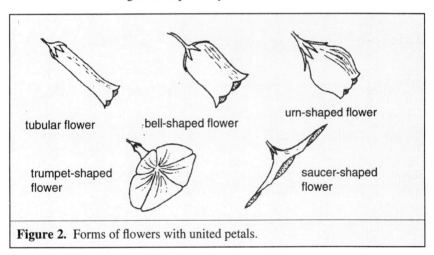

tubular flower

bell-shaped flower

urn-shaped flower

trumpet-shaped flower

saucer-shaped flower

Figure 2. Forms of flowers with united petals.

Stamens are usually separate, but in some species all or some are united into a ring encircling the pistil. Stamens may be fused by their filaments or by their anthers. The pistil, too, may be composed of several united units, called **carpels**. Most often, carpels are united by their ovaries so that the base of the pistil is several chambered, the number usually corresponding to the number of carpels. The number of carpels in a compound pistil is often reflected in the number of styles or lobes of the stigma.

Flower Symmetry

If all the petals of a flower are alike in size and shape, and all the sepals likewise are similar, the flower is said to be **regular**. When viewed from above, a regular flower can be divided into mirror-image halves by any of several imaginary planes passed through its center; that is, a regular flower exhibits radial symmetry. An example of a regular flower is shown in figure 3.

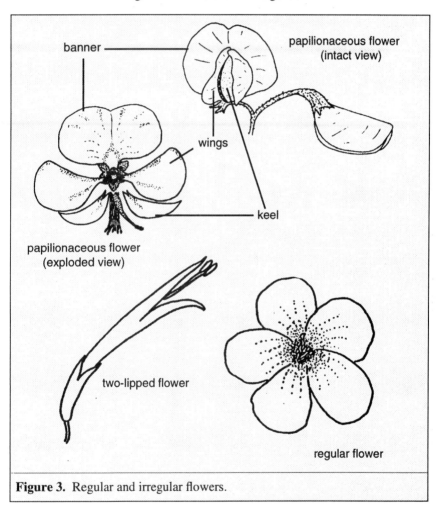

banner

papilionaceous flower (intact view)

wings

keel

papilionaceous flower (exploded view)

two-lipped flower

regular flower

Figure 3. Regular and irregular flowers.

A flower in which one or more of the petals or sepals are distinctly different in size or shape from the rest is said to be **irregular**. Such a flower has only a single imaginary plane that can be passed through its center to produce mirror-image halves. Irregular flowers take many forms. Many are distinctly **two-lipped**, some of the petals or sepals grouped on the upper side of the flower, the remainder on the lower side. Another common arrangement is that found in many members of the pea family (Fabaceae). Pea flowers possess five petals, each given a specific name. The rearmost petal is the largest and is called the **banner**. The banner is flanked by two smaller petals, called **wings**. At the front of the flower between the wings is a pair of smaller petals that are fused into a boatshaped **keel**. The keel encloses the reproductive parts of the flower. Flowers with this arrangement are said to be **papilionaceous**. Examples of both types of irregular flowers are shown in figure 3.

Relationship of Flower Parts

In most flowers, the floral parts of adjacent whorls are attached independently to the receptacle and alternate in position with the parts of neighboring whorls. That is, the petals alternate with the sepals, the stamens alternate with the petals, and the carpels (if several in number) alternate with the stamens. Deviation from this pattern is often a clue to a plant's affinities and identity. Stamens, for instance, are opposite the petals in some flowers. They may even be attached to the petals rather than to the receptacle, especially when the petals are united. When stamens are attached to the petals, their filaments usually are short or missing altogether. Deviations from the usual arrangement occur among other floral parts as well.

The placement of the ovary with respect to the petals and sepals is sometimes critical in classification. If the sepals and petals attach at the base of the ovary so that the entire ovary is above their point of attachment, the ovary is said to be **superior**. An ovary that is at least partially below the attachment site of the petals and sepals is said to be **inferior**. In some flowers, an expansion of the receptacle, called the **disc**, surrounds the basal part of the ovary. Often when a disc is present, the calyx and disc are fused into a cup-shaped **receptocalyx**. This is typical, for instance, of the rose family (Rosaceae).

Number of Floral Parts

The number of floral parts in each set varies considerably from one species to the next, but it is common for petals, stamens and pistils to occur in multiples of the sepal number. In a flower with four sepals, for example, there are generally four (or 8, 12, 16, etc.) petals, stamens, and pistils.

Two large groupings (orders) of flowering plants are based, in part, on the number of floral parts. Members of order Dicotyledonae (dicots) typically have flower parts in multiples of 4 or 5; the floral parts of plants belonging to the order Monocotyledonae (monocots), in contrast, are usually in multiples of 3. However, the number of floral parts does not always follow the predicted pattern. Pistils, in particular, often are reduced in number, only one or two in a 4- or 5-partite flower. A reduction in the expected number of stamens is less common.

Inflorescences

Plant identification is often dependent on the arrangement of the flowers on the flowering shoot. In some plants, flowers are widely separated from one another, each one situated alone at the end of a branch or in the axil of a leaf. Such flowers are said to be **solitary**. In other species, flowers occur in clusters on a flower shoot; such a grouping is called an **inflorescence**. Inflorescences take a variety of arrangements, the more common of which are shown diagrammatically in figure 4.

One type of inflorescence, the **composite head**, is of particular importance since it forms the basis for membership in the large sunflower family (Asteraceae). The "flower" of a sunflower plant is, in reality, not one flower but a *collection* of many tiny tubular flowers, the entire mass underlain by a series of leaflike bracts (figure 5). The flowers that constitute a typical sunflower head take two forms. Those in the center, or **disc**, of the head are regular and are called **disc flowers**. Around the head's periphery the flowers are irregular, one corolla lobe elongated into a petallike structure called a **ray** or **ligule**; these are **ray flowers**. Although both disc and ray flowers occur in sunflower heads, the heads of some species of plants are composed entirely of disc flowers, other entirely of ray flowers. The bracts that underlie a composite head are referred to as **phyllaries** or **involucral bracts**; all the phyllaries together make up the **involucre**.

Fertilization and Fruits

When pollen is passed from an anther to the sticky surface of a stigma of the same or different flower fertilization may occur. On the stigma, a pollen grain forms a tunnel within the style to an ovule below. When a male reproductive cell migrates through the tunnel to an ovule, fertilization occurs. The fertilized ovule becomes a seed and the ovary wall becomes the fruit.

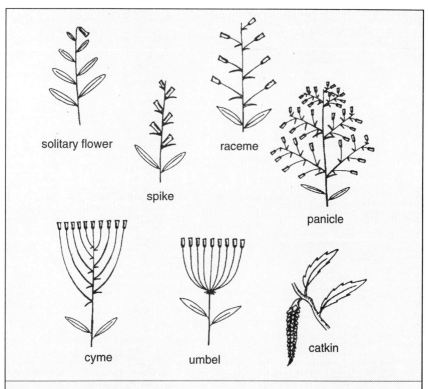

Figure 4. Common inflorescences.

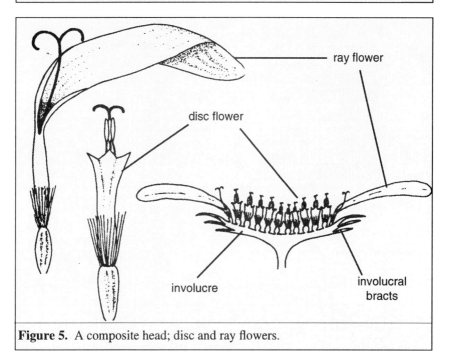

Figure 5. A composite head; disc and ray flowers.

Fruits come in a variety of forms: drupes, achenes, berries, nuts, capsules, legumes, and so forth. Since fruit characters are not generally used in our keys, they are not discussed further here. All are defined in the glossary.

Monoecious and Dioecious Plants

The flowers of most plants contain both the male and the female reproductive parts; such flowers are said to be **perfect**. In some species, flowers are **unisexual**, the stamens in one flower, the pistils in another. When male and female flowers of a unisexual species occur on the same plant, the species is said to be **monoecious** ("one household"); those species in which the male and female flowers occur on separate plants are called **dioecious** ("two households").

Cones

Not all reproductive structures of plants are borne in flowers. The reproductive organs of pine trees, for example, are housed in **cones** (figure 6). The familiar woody pine cones contain only the female sex organs and produce the seeds. Male cones are usually quite small and inconspicuous; instead of being woody, they are papery and disintegrate easily, releasing their abundant male sex cells, or pollen, to the wind.

A female pine cone consists of many whorls of woody **scales** spiraling around a central axis. On the surface of each scale, near the axis, two ovules arise on papery bracts. When the ovules are fertilized by pollen, they become the seeds. The seeds are released when the scales separate and the cone opens.

The cones of many cone-bearing plants are not woody and bear little resemblance to pine cones. For example, the "berries" of a juniper tree are actually female cones with soft, fleshy scales. In the related cypresses, the fleshy berries become woody as they mature. In the more primitive ephedras (Mormon tea), the ovules and pollen sacs (anthers) are borne naked on short, soft bracts in the leaf axil.

Pines and their allies are monoecious, the male and female cones being borne on the same plants. Junipers and ephedras, on the other hand, usually are dioecious, the female cones on one plant, the male cones on another.

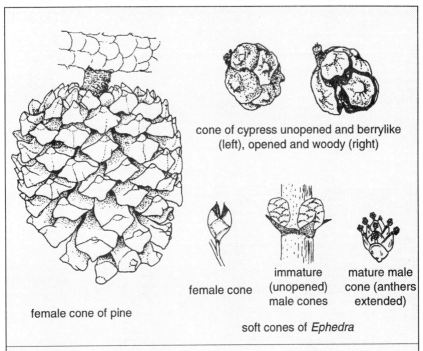

cone of cypress unopened and berrylike (left), opened and woody (right)

female cone of pine

female cone

immature (unopened) male cones

mature male cone (anthers extended)

soft cones of *Ephedra*

Figure 6. Structure of cones

Leaves and stems

Leaves and stems are somewhat more variable than flowers and cones, but they, too, provide many characters useful in separating plant groups. Here we consider only the points of critical concern in the use of this book.

Simple Leaves

A typical leaf consists of two parts, a stalk or **petiole**, and a **blade**. In some leaves the blade attaches directly to the branch, there being no clear cut petiole; such a leaf is said to be **sessile**. The point where a leaf attaches to a stem is called a **node**.

The leaf blade is permeated by a network of veins, the arrangement of which often serves to identify plants species. Leaves with many equally prominent veins running lengthwise through the blade are said to be **parallel-veined**. If a blade has a single prominent vein running from the base with less obvious veins branching off it like the barbs of a feather, the leaf is said to be **pinnately-veined**. Leaves with three of more equally

11

prominent veins arising from the base and spreading outward like the lines on the palm of one's hand are said to be **palmately-veined.** Examples of these venation types are shown in figure 7.

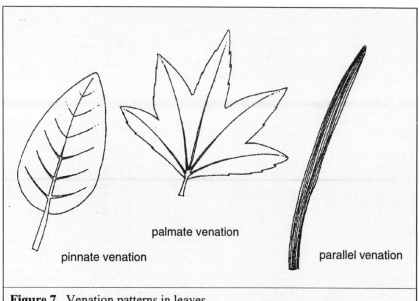

palmate venation

pinnate venation

parallel venation

Figure 7. Venation patterns in leaves.

Compound Leaves

A leaf that has a single blade is said to be **simple.** One that is divided into several leaflike units, called **leaflets** or **pinnae,** is said to be **compound.** Since leaves always have buds in their axil, the easiest way to determine if a leaf is simple or compound is to look for a bud where the petiole joins the stem. If no bud is found, the "leaf" is a leaflet, a subunit of a compound leaf.

A compound leaf is said to be **pinnately-compound** if its leaflets arise in series along a single main axis, or **rachis.** If all the leaflets arise from a single point at the end of the petiole, the leaf is **palmately-compound.** Some compound leaves are doubly divided, the leaflets themselves composed of still smaller leaflets (called **pinnules**). A doubly compound leaf with pinnately arranged leaflets and pinnules is said to be **bipinnately compound.** Examples of compound leaves are shown in figure 8.

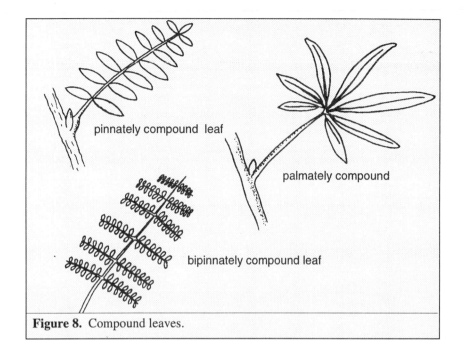

Figure 8. Compound leaves.

Leaf Arrangements

The arrangement of leaves along the stem is also important in plant identification. Most commonly, leaves **alternate** along the stem, a leaf on one side followed by a leaf on the other side. Less commonly, leaves arise in pairs, one on either side of the stem; such leaves are said to be **opposite**. Still less frequently, leaves are **whorled**, appearing in groups of three or more at the same node. These arrangements are shown in figure 9.

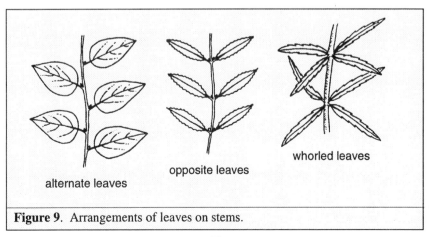

Figure 9. Arrangements of leaves on stems.

13

Plant names

Most common plants, especially trees and shrubs, are known to many persons by a common name, black cottonwood or red willow, for example. Unfortunately, such names are not standardized and tend to vary from one individual to another and one region to another. Thus, a plant that one person knows as jojoba another may know as goatnut, another as quinine plant, another as lemonleaf, and still another as pignut. Obviously, the use of so many names for the same plant — or the same name for different plants, another common occurrence — can lead to great confusion.

Scientific Names

Because miscommunication is possible when using common, or vernacular, names, scientists always rely on standardized names. Each kind, or *species*, of plant is assigned a name that applies to it alone, thus assuring accurate communication. Moreover, the name applied to a given plant is the same the world over, no matter what the language of the people. Although we use common names in this book, each plant is also identified by its scientific name. When referring to another work, always use the scientific name!

By international convention, all names used by scientists consist of two parts; that is, they are *binomials*. In scientific circles, a white oak, for instance, is properly called *Quercus alba*, and a ponderosa pine, *Pinus ponderosa*. Each binomial is much like the first and last name of a person, except that the order is the reverse of that in standard English: the second part of a scientific name is the equivalent of a person's given name, James or Judy; the first part is more like a surname and identifies the larger group to which a species belongs.

Scientific names are always written in Latin. In print, they are italicized or underlined, thereby setting them apart. It is also standard practice to capitalize the first (group) name but to begin the second (specific) name with a lower case letter. Botanists, however, permit exceptions if the second name was derived from a proper noun, for instance, as in *Populus Fremontii,* a tree named after John Charles Fremont, a soldier, explorer and amateur botanist. In this book, however, we consistently use lower case letters for the second name.

To facilitate organizing plant species and to more readily show relationships, botanists place closely related species into ever more inclusive groups. Very similar species are placed into the same genus; similar genera (the plural of genus), in turn, are put together in the same family, and so on. Thus, *Quercus kelloggii, Quercus chrysolepis,* and *Quercus agrifolia* are all oaks and belong to the same genus: *Quercus.* All the oaks, however, are similar in certain respects to the beech trees; consequently, all are placed in the family Fagaceae (beech family). In this book we include the name of the family to which each plant belongs so that relationships can more readily be determined. Family names are always capitalized and end in -aceae (some older family names, e.g. Compositae, Leguminosae, Labiatae, have now been replaced with Asteraceae, Fabaceae, and Lamiaceae, respectively).

As botanists come to know the plant species better, the scientific names are occasionally changed. This occurs, for instance, when what was originally thought to be one species turns out to be two or more, or when populations thought to be distinct species are found on careful study to be so similar that they must be considered a single species. In this book we have, for the most part, used the names to be found in Hickman's *The Jepson Manual: Higher Plants of California,* the most recent (1993) standard reference published on southern California botany.

Extent of coverage

The plants included in this book are those to be found in the deserts of southern California — both the Mojave Desert and the Colorado Desert — and on the mountain slopes fringing the deserts to an elevation of approximately 5000 feet. The northern terminus of coverage has been set arbitrarily at the northern borders of Kern and San Bernardino Counties. Thus, the Death Valley region is not covered, although many of the plants included in this book also occur in that area. The Mexican border and the Colorado River form the southern and eastern limits of the book's coverage. Figure 10 indicates the area included.

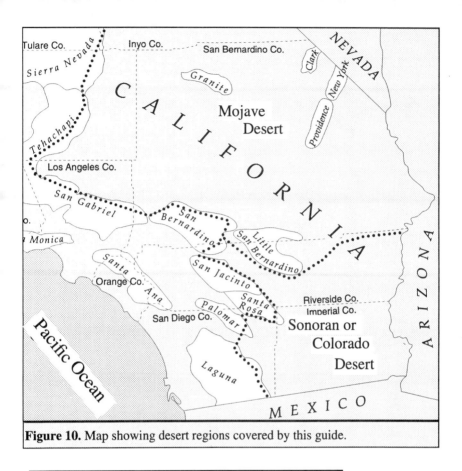

Figure 10. Map showing desert regions covered by this guide.

Desert plant communities

Each plant community is a unique assemblage of species. Although hundreds of species may be present, certain ones are more obvious, more abundant, and more common than others. These species are called *dominants* and, as the name implies, are more influential than others. By their very size and abundance they change the environment for other species, creating shade or quickly absorbing moisture from the soil. In this way, they make it possible for some species to survive with them, but force others to grow elsewhere.

Still other plants, less commonly seen, are nevertheless characteristic of a given plant community, their presence quite literally identifying it. For this reason, they are called *indicator species*. Below are listed the plant communities of the deserts of southern California, together with a

16

listing of the characteristic shrubs and trees of each; information presented has been modified from a listing presented by Munz and Keck in *A California Flora* (1959). Throughout the text the communities are referenced by their abbreviations.

Creosote Bush Scrub (CBS)

On well-drained soils of alluvial fans and gentle slopes. Below 3500' throughout both deserts. **Creosote bush** (*Larrea tridentata*), **Burro-weed** (*Ambrosia dumosa*), **Ocotillo** (*Fouquieria splendens*), **Mojave** and **Schott indigo bush,** and **Smoke tree** (*Psorothamnus arborescens, P. schottii, P. spinosus*), **Desert thorn** and **Anderson desert thorn** (*Lycium brevipes, L. andersonii*), **Burrobrush** (*Hymenoclea salsola*), **Brittlebush** and **Bush encelia** (*Encelia farinosa, E. frutescens*), **Apricot mallow** (*Sphaeralcea ambigua*), **Squaw waterweed** (*Baccharis sergiloides*), **Beavertail cactus, Teddy-bear** and **Silver cholla** (*Opuntia basilaris, O. bigelovii, O. echinocarpa*).

Joshua Tree Woodland (JTW)

On well-drained slopes and flatlands. Between 2500 and 4000' throughout the Mojave Desert. **Joshua tree** (*Yucca brevifolia*), **California** and **Utah juniper** (*Juniperus californica, J. osteosperma*), **Bladder sage** (*Salazaria mexicana*), **Anderson desert thorn** and **Boxthorn** (*Lycium andersonii, L. cooperi*), **California buckwheat** (*Eriogonum fasciculatum*), **Cotton-thorn, Little** and **Mojave horsebrush** (*Tetradymia axillaris, T. glabrata, T. stenolepis*).

Pinyon Pine — Juniper Woodland (PJW)

On desert-facing mountain slopes from the Tehachapis southward and in higher mountains of the Mojave Desert; mostly between Sagebrush Scrub or Joshua Tree Woodland and Yellow Pine Forest, from 4000 to 8000'. **Singleleaf pinyon pine** (*Pinus monophylla*), **Calif.** and **Utah juniper** (*Juniperus californica, J. osteosperma*), **Muller's, Tucker's** and **Scrub live oak** (*Quercus cornelius-mulleri, Q. john-tuckeri, Q. turbinella*), **Antelope bush** and **Cliff rose** (*Purshia tridentata, P. mexicana*), **Apache plume** (*Fallugia paradoxa*), **Curl-leaf mountain mahogany** (*Cercocarpus ledifolius*), **Mojave** and **Banana yucca** (*Yucca schidigera, Y. baccata*).

Sagebrush Scrub (SbS)

On deep, permeable soils. Mainly between 4000 and 7500' on the mountains fringing the western edge of the Mojave Desert, from the Sierra Nevadas south to the San

Bernardino Mountains; also on the mountains bordering the Colorado Desert in San Diego County. **Big** and **Black sagebrush** *(Artemisia tridentata, A. nova)*, **Blackbush** *(Coleogyne ramosissima)*, **Rubber** and **Yellow rabbitbrush** *(Chrysothamnus nauseosus, C. viscidiflorus)*, **Shadscale** and **Fourwing saltbush** *(Atriplex confertifolia, A. canescens)*, **Cotton-thorn** *(Tetradymia axillaris)*, **Antelope bush** *(Purshia tridentata)*.

Alkali Sink (AIS) On poorly drained alkaline soils and dry lake beds on the Mojave Desert floor. **Allscale, Spinescale, Big** and **Parry saltbush** *(Atriplex polycarpa, A. spinifera, A. lentiformis, A. parryi)*, **Iodine bush** *(Allenrolfea occidentalis)*, **Bush seepweed** *(Suaeda moquinii)*.

Shadscale Scrub (SsS) On heavy soils, usually underlain by an impermeable hardpan. Flatlands of the Mojave Desert, from 3000 to 6000'. **Shadscale** *(Atriplex confertifolia)*, **Hop-sage** *(Grayia spinosa)*, **Winter fat** *(Krascheninnikovia lanata)*, **Budsage** *(Artemisia spinescens)*, **Greenfire** *(Menodora spinescens)*, **Broom matchweed** *(Gutierrezia sarothrae)*, **Blackbush** *(Coleogyne ramosissima)*.

Riparian Woodland (RiW) Along watercourses throughout many other communities. Species composition varies but on the desert floor commonly includes: **Honey mesquite** *(Prosopis glandulosa)*, **Smoke tree** *(Psorothamnus spinosus)*, **Blue palo verde** *(Cercidium floridum)*, **Ironwood** *(Olneya tesota)*, **Arrowweed** *(Pluchea sericea)* and **Desert-willow** *(Chilopsis linearis)*.

Many species considered in this book are also found outside the deserts in other plant communities. Those outlying plant communities referenced by their abbreviations in this text include: **Chaparral (Cha), Coastal Sage Scrub (CSS), Southern Oak Woodland (SOW), Valley Grassland (VGr), Coastal Strand (CoS), Coastal Salt Marsh (CSM), Yellow Pine Forest (YPF),** and **Foothill Woodland (FhW)**.

Begin here

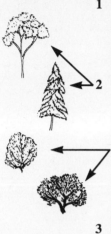

1   A—Plant a **Cactus,** that is, it lacks leaves and has succulent stems with clusters of spines and/or tiny barbed hairs . . . . Go to **Key A: Cacti**, this page.
      B—Plant not a cactus. . . . . Go to 2

2   A—Plant a **Tree,** that is, it has a single main stem (trunk) from which secondary branches arise well above the ground, and plant is 10 feet tall or taller when mature . . . . Go to **Key B**: **Trees,** page 20
      B—Plant a **Shrub,** that is, it arises from the ground either as a cluster of branches or as a short trunk that branches low to the ground (or not at all), and when mature is typically less than 15 feet tall . . . Go to 3

3   A—**Flowers** or (rarely) soft **Cones** present . . . .
      . . . . . . Go to **Key C: Shrubs in Flower,** page 23
      B—Flowers or cones lacking . . . .
      . . . . Go to **Key D: Shrubs not in Flower,** page 36
      [NOTE: Key D permits identification of shrubs when they are not flowering. Because vegetative characters are more variable than are flower characters, positive identification with Key D is often difficult. Key C is more precise; use it whenever possible.]

Key A: Cacti (Family Cactaceae)

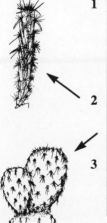

1   A—Stems divided into distinctive sections connected one to the other in linear or branching sequence; fine, barbed, hair-like spines (glochids) present, typically at base of larger spines . . . . Go to 2
      B—Stems not in sections; glochids lacking . . . Go to 4

2   A—Branch sections round in cross-section . . . .
      . . . . **Chollas** *(Opuntia),* page 134
      B—Branch sections flattened . . . . Go to 3

3   A—Spines present . . **Prickly pears** *(Opuntia),* page 136
      B—Spines absent; clusters of glochids scattered over branch segments . . . .
      . . **Beavertail cactus** *(Opuntia basilaris),* page 137

4   **A**—Trunk with 12-24 lengthwise ribs; spines straight; older plants with from one to several upright arms . . . . **Saguaro** *(Carnegiea gigantea)*, page 138

        B—Trunk with 20-30 lengthwise ribs; spines twisted, hooked, with circular rings; unbranched . . . **Calif. barrel cactus** *(Ferocactus cylindraceus)*, page 139

Key B: Trees

1   **A**—Leaves present . . . . Go to 2

        B—Leaves absent . . . . Go to 23

2   **A**—Leaves dagger-like, sharp-tipped, 10-12" long, in spreading tufts at branch ends . . . . **Joshua tree** *(Yucca brevifolia)*, page 54

        B—Leaves not as above . . . . Go to 3

3   **A**—Leaves stiff, needle-like, occurring singly or in bundles of 2 or 4, a papery sheath at base of each bundle (or single needle); seeds borne in woody cones . . . . **Pinyon pines** (Pinus), page 133 *[If tree bears what appear to be small woody cones, but its leaves are broad and flat, not needle-like, it is White alder and the"cones" are woody catkins!]*

        B—Leaves not stiff needles; seeds borne from flowers or soft, berrylike cones . . . . Go to 4

4   **A**—Leaves small (mostly less than 1/4" long), scale-like, closely pressed to and obscuring the stem *[Be careful here! If tree appears to have long, drooping, filamentous leaves, check them carefully with a hand-lens; those "leaves" may be small branchlets entirely encased in tiny scale-like leaves.]* . . Go to 5

        B—Leaves broad, flat, simple or compound; reproduction by means of flowers . . . . Go to 6

5   **A**—Leaves in 4 or 6 rows, those on young stems sharp-pointed; reproduction by means of berry-like cones of 2-6 fleshy scales . **Junipers** *(Juniperus)*, page 132

        B—Scale-like leaves tiny, not in rows, closely wrapped around thin terminal branchlets; reproduction by means of flowers . . **Tamarisk** *(Tamarix)*, page 70

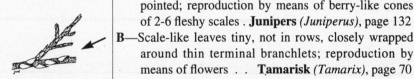

6 **A**—Leaves compound . . . . Go to 7
    B—Leaves simple . . . . Go to 12

7 **A**—Leaves twice pinnately compound . . . . . . Go to 8
    [Check several leaves; petioles often are so short
    that the two leaflets, each with many pinnules, seem
    to arise separately from stem.]
    B—Leaves once pinnately compound . . . . . . Go to 9

8 **A**—Bark of branches distinctly green . . . .
    . . . . **Palo verde** *(Cercidium)*, page 73
    B—Bark not green . . . . **Mesquite** *(Prosopis)*, page 72

9 **A**—Leaflets tiny, alternating along a flat, green rachis
    that may reach 12" and persist after leaflets have
    fallen; spines in 3's, reddish; bark of branches green .
    . . **Mex. palo verde** *(Parkinsonia aculeata)*, page 78
    B—Leaflets opposite; rachis not flat; spines, if present,
    not in 3's; bark not green . . . . Go to 10

10 **A**—Leaves with an even number of leaflets, there being
    no unpaired leaflet at the tip . . . .
    . . . . **Ironwood** *(Olneya tesota)*, page 77
    B—Leaflets odd numbered, an unpaired leaflet at the tip
    . . . . Go to 11

11 **A**—Leaflets notched or toothed . . . .
    . . . . . . **Velvet ash** *(Fraxinus velutina)*, page 124
    B—Edges of leaflets smooth . . . .
    . . . **Elephant tree** *(Bursera microphylla)*, page 62

12 **A**—Leaves palmately veined . . . . Go to 13
    B—Leaves pinnately veined . . . . Go to 15

13 **A**—Leaves many feet long, fan-shaped, clustered at the
    top of a thick, unbranched trunk, the petiole edged
    with curved hooks . . . .
    . . **Calif. fan palm** *(Washingtonia filifera)*, page 53
    B—Leaves not as above . . . . Go to 14

14 **A**—Older leaves 6-8" across, 3- to 5-lobed, lobes longer
    than wide . . . .
    . **Western sycamore** *(Platanus racemosa)*, page 69
    B—Mature leaves 3/8" to 1 1/2" across, 3 lobed, each
    lobe wider than long . . . . **Flannel**
    bush *(Fremontodendron californicum)*, page 116

15 | A—Leaves opposite. . . . .
. . . . **Singleleaf ash** *(Fraxinus anomala)*, page 124
B—Leaves alternate . . . . Go to 16

16 | A—Leaf edges smooth . . . . Go to 17
B—Leaf edges toothed or lobed . . . . Go to 22

17 | A—Plant spinose, the tips of older branches sharp and
spiny. Go to 18
B—Branches blunt-tipped, not spinose. . . . . Go to 20

18 | A—Leaves few, occurring singly on gray or gray-green,
gland-dotted branches . . . .
. . . **Smoke tree** *(Psorothamnus spinosus)*, page 75
B—Leaves abundant, clustered at tips of short, spurlike
branchlets . . . . Go to 19

19 | A—Leaves narrow, rarely exceeding 1/4" in width,
broadest near the tip. . . . .
. . . . **Desert almond** *(Prunus fasciculata)*, page 59
B—Leaves oval, 1/4–1/2" wide, broadest at or below the
middle . . . . **Lotebush** *(Ziziphus parryi)*, page 65

20 | A—Leaves less than 1 1/2" long, leathery, the edges
rolled under, on short, spurlike branchlets . . . . . .
. . . . **Mountain mahogany** *(Cercocarpus)*, page 62
B—Leaves commonly 2" long or longer, thin, flat, not on
spurs . . . . Go to 21

21 | A—Leaves mostly 2 to 4" long, often 1/2" wide or more .
. . **Goodding's willow** *(Salix gooddingii)*, page 126
B—Leaves 4 to 6" long, of nearly uniform 1/4" width
throughout, sickle-shaped, pointed at both ends . . .
. . . . . **Desert-willow** *(Chilopsis linearis)*, page 87

22 | A—Leaf somewhat triangular, about as broad as long . .
Fremont cottonwood *(Populus fremontii)*, page 125
B—Leaf ovalish, about twice as long as broad . . . . . .
. . . . . **White alder** *(Alnus rhombifolia)*, page 128

23 | A—Plant strongly scented; trunk thick, swollen, the bark
red-brown; branches lack sharp spines. . . . .
. . . **Elephant tree** *(Bursera microphylla)*, page 62
B—Plant not strongly scented; bark not red-brown;
branches either sharp-tipped or armed with spines or
thorns . . . . Go to 24

24 | A—Bark green . . . . **Palo verde** *(Cercidium)*, page 73
B—Bark not green . . . . Go to 25

25 | A—Spines at intervals along branches; branches themselves blunt-ended . . . .
. . . . **Mesquite** *(Prosopis)*, page 72
B—Spines lacking along branches, but terminal branchlets spine-tipped . . . .
. . . **Smoke tree** *(Psorothamnus spinosus)*, page 75

Key C: Shrubs in Flower

1 | A—Plant with true flowers . . . . Go to 2
B—Fleshy, sometimes berry-like cones (strobili) present, not flowers . . . . Go to 6

2 | A—Petals lacking . . . .
. . . . . . Go to **Key C - 3: Petals Absent**, page 28
B—Petals present . . . . Go to 3

3 | A—Petals and sepals in multiples of 3 AND major leaf veins run lengthwise, parallel to each other . . . . .
. . . Go to **Key C - 1: Shrubby Monocots**, page 24
B—Petals and sepals in multiples of 4 or 5; leaf veins not parallel . . . . Go to 4

4 | A—Flowers in few- to many-flowered heads; heads underlain by leaflike or papery bracts (= involucre) .
. . . . Go to **Key C - 2: Flowers in Heads**, page 24
B—Flowers not in heads with an involucre . . . Go to 5

5 | A—Petals united into a tubular, funnel-, urn-, trumpet-, or saucer-shaped corolla . . . .
. . . . . . Go to **Key C - 4: Petals United**, page 30
B—Petals separate or mostly so *[take this choice if petals are joined only at base, or if only a single pair of petals is fused]* . . . .
. . . . . Go to **Key C - 5: Petals Separate**, page 32

6 | A—Plant appears leafless but has pairs or triplets of tiny scalelike leaves at widely spaced intervals along the stems . . . . **Desert tea** *(Ephedra)*, page 130
B—Terminal branches covered with scale-like leaves, those on youngest branches sharp pointed . . . . . .
. . . . **Juniper** *(Juniperus)*, page 132

Key C - 1: Shrubby Monocots

1 A—Leaves thick, fleshy with sharp, curved spines along
edges, growing in a rosette directly on ground;
flowers yellow or greenish; ovary inferior . . . . . .
. . . . **Century plant** *(Agave deserti)*, page 57
  B—Leaves long, narrow, either stiff and dagger-like or
flexible and grass-like (but not fleshy), without
spines on edges; leaves in rosettes at tips of
branches, at top of short trunk, or directly on ground;
flowers purplish or white; ovary superior . . Go to 2

2 A—Perianth (petals + sepals) less than 1/4" long,
whitish; flowers may be bisexual, male or female;
leaves somewhat flexible, grass-like, usually lacking
a distinct spine at tip . . . **Nolina** *(Nolina)*, page 56
  B—Perianth 1-6" long, cream-white or purplish; flowers
bisexual (perfect); leaves stiff, dagger-like, spine-
tipped . . . . **Yuccas** *(Yucca)*, page 55

Key C - 2: Flowers in Heads (Asteraceae)

1 A—Corollas all distinctly 2-lipped, the 3-toothed outer
lobe longer than the 2-toothed inner lobe . . . . . .
. . . . **California trixis** *(Trixis californica)*, page 99
  B—Corollas not all distinctly 2-lipped . . . . . . Go to 2

2 A—Heads with disc flowers only . . . .
. . Go to **Key C - 2.1: Disc Flowers Only**, this page
  B—Heads with both ray and disc flowers . . . .
. Go to **Key C - 2.2: Ray and Disc Flowers**, page 26

Key C-2.1:
Disc
Flowers
Only

1 A—Flowers blue or purple . . . .
. . . . . . **Arrowweed** *(Pluchea sericea)*, page 112
  B—Flowers yellow, white or faintly purplish . . Go to 2

2 A—Plant nearly leafless or leaves reduced to scales . . .
. . . . Go to 3
  B—Plant distinctly leafy, its leaves not scale-like . . . .
. . . . Go to 4

3 **A**—A broom-like shrub with mostly erect branches; leaves scale-like, less than 3/8″ long . . . .
Scale-broom *(Lepidospartum squamatum)*, page 115
B—A low, rounded, much-branched shrub, its thin branches extending in all directions; leafless or with a few threadlike leaves here and there . . . .
. . . . **Sweet bush** *(Bebbia juncea)*, page 99

4 **A**—Leaves stiff, needle-like, aromatic, in tufts at branch ends . . . .
. . **Pygmy-cedar** *(Peucephyllum schottii)*, page 101
B—Leaves not stiff, not needle-like; aromatic or not . . .
. . . . Go to 5

5 **A**—Flowers bright yellow . . . . Go to 6
B—Flowers whitish or very pale yellow . . . . Go to 11

6 **A**—Involucres of 4-7 bracts in a single row; stems densely covered with a mat of wool; plant often spiny
. . . . **Horsebrush** *(Tetradymia)*, page 96
B—Involucres of more than 7 bracts in several rows; stems not densely woolly; plant not spiny . . Go to 7

7 **A**—Heads narrow, mostly 5-flowered (occasionally up to 8) . . . . . **Rabbitbrush** *(Chrysothamnus)*, page 106
B—Heads with many more than 8 flowers . . . . Go to 8

8 **A**—Involucral bracts arranged in 4 horizontal rows or ranks; bracts broad, whitish with green tips, the edges papery and/or fringed with hairs . . . .
Goldenhead *(Acamptopappus sphaerocephalus)*, page 98
B—Involucral bracts in several rows, overlapping like shingles . . . . Go to 9

9 **A**—Leaves covered with stiff hairs with blister-like swellings at the base, rough to the touch . . . .
. . . . . . **Bush encelia** *(Encelia frutescens)*, page 94
B—Leaves without stiff hairs swollen at base, usually not markedly rough to the touch . . . . Go to 10

10 **A**—Leaf edges irregularly toothed . . . .
Pale-leaf goldenbush *(Isocoma acradenia)*, page 103
B—Leaf edges smooth . . . .
. . . . **Goldenbush** *(Ericameria)*, page 102

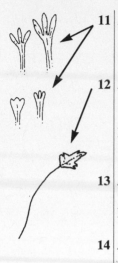

11 A—Leaves aromatic, 3-toothed at apex . . . .
. . . . **Sagebrush** *(Artemisia),* page 104
B—Leaves not aromatic, not 3-toothed . . . . . Go to 12

12 A—Petiole many times longer than leaf blade; leaves opposite in lower parts of plant, alternate above . . .
. . . **Arrowleaf** *(Pleurocoronis pluriseta),* page 112
B—Petiole shorter than blade; leaves alternate (rarely opposite) . . . . Go to 13

13 A—Two distinctly different kinds of heads (male and female) present on the same plant . . . . . Go to 14
B—Each plant with a single kind of head . . . Go to 15

14 A—Leaves thread-like; male and female heads in same leaf axil; female heads 1-flowered, their involucral bracts broad, papery, many, persisting in fruit . . . .
. . . . **Burrobrush** *(Hymenoclea salsola),* page 100
B—Leaves not thread-like, the edges toothed or lobed; male heads on top branches, female heads on lower; bracts of 1-flowered female heads with prickles, becoming a bur . . . .
. . . . **Bursage** or **Burro-weed** *(Ambrosia),* page 93

15 A—Heads with flowers all of a single sex, male and female heads on different plants; involucral bracts green and leaflike . **Baccharis** *(Baccharis),* page 110
B—Heads with perfect flowers (i.e., all flowers with both stamens and pistil); involucral bracts papery, membranous, not leaflike . . . .
. . . . **Brickellbush** *(Brickellia),* page 108

**Key C-2.2:
Ray and
Disc
Flowers**

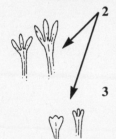

1 A—Ray flowers mostly 9 or fewer . . . . Go to 2
B—Ray flowers mostly 10 or more . . . . Go to 5

2 A—Leaves strongly aromatic, 3-toothed at apex or palmately 3-7 lobed, each lobe ending in 3 smaller lobes . . . . **Sagebrush** *(Artemisia),* page 104
B—Leaves not strongly aromatic . . . . Go to 3

3 A—Only about 5 involucral bracts present . . . .
Golden yarrow *(Eriophyllum confertiflorum),* page 113
B—Many more than 5 involucral bracts present . Go to 4

4 A—Disc flowers mostly fewer than 6 . . . .
. . . . Matchweed *(Gutierrezia)*, page 114
B—Disc flowers mostly more than 6 . . . .
. . . . Goldenbush *(Ericameria)*, page 102

5 A—Involucral bracts elongate and in a single series, a
few long, conspicuous bractlets at the base; leaves
1–4" long, divided into 5–9 linear lobes . . . . . .
. . . Bush groundsel *(Senecio flaccidus)*, page 113
B—Involucral bracts and leaves not as above . . Go to 6

6 A—Leaves mostly 1/8" or less wide, 5 or more times as
long; edges of involucral bracts thin, white, papery .
. . . . Go to 7
B—Leaves mostly 1/8" or more wide; involucral bracts
not as above . . . . Go to 8

7 A—Leaves resinous, dotted with conspicuous glands;
involucre 1/4–3/8" high; widespread . . . .
. . . . Goldenbush *(Ericameria)*, page 102
B—Leaves not resinous or gland-dotted; involucre about
1/4" tall; plant of eastern Mojave Desert mountains.
. . . . **Shockley
goldenhead** *(Acamptopappus shockleyi)*, page 98

8 A—Leaves distinctly rough to the touch, the edges
distinctly toothed; lower leaves opposite . . . . . .
. . . Desert sunflower *(Viguiera parishii)*, page 100
B—Leaves not rough-feeling, the edges smooth; leaves
alternate . . . . **Brittlebush** *(Encelia farinosa)*
or **Virginia City encelia** *(E. virginensis)*, page 94

Key C - 3 : Petals Absent (or apparently so)

1 A—Male flowers (and usually female as well) arranged in catkins . . . .
. . Go to **Key C - 3.1, Flowers in Catkins,** this page
B—Flowers not in catkins . . . .
Go to **Key C - 3.2, Flowers not in Catkins,** this page

Key C - 3.1:
Flowers in **1** A—Leaves compound . . **Mesquite** *(Prosopis)*, page 22
Catkins *[Uh-oh! You made a major mistake! What you thought were catkins on this plant are really spikes; i.e., the flowers are perfect, with both male and female parts.]*
B—Leaves simple . . . . Go to 2

2 A—Leaves opposite . **Silk tassel bush** *(Garrya)*, page 129
B—Leaves alternate . . . . Go to 3

3 A—Only male flowers in catkins, the female flowers solitary or in clusters of 3; fruit an acorn . . . . . .
. . . . **Desert oaks** *(Quercus)*, page 128
B—Flowers of both sexes in catkins; fruit a capsule bearing seeds with tufts of long white hairs . . . . .
. . . . **Willows** *(Salix)*, page 127

Key C - 3.2:
Flowers Not **1** A—Leaves palmately veined, 3- to 11-lobed . . Go to 2
in Catkins B—Leaves pinnately veined . . . . Go to 3

2 A—Sepals large, yellow, petal-like; mature leaves mostly 3" or less across, with 3 - 5 rounded lobes; petiole attached to leaf edge . . . . **Flannel bush** *(Fremontodendron californicum)*, page 116
B—Sepals small, green; leaves with 5 - 11 pointed lobes; mature leaves 6" or more across; petiole attached to lower leaf surface . . . .
. . . . . **Castor bean** *(Ricinus communis)*, page 117

3 A—Leaves opposite . . . . Go to 4
B—Leaves alternate . . . . Go to 6

4 A—Leaves 1/2" long or less, in opposite clusters (fascicles); stamens 20-40 . . . .
. . . **Blackbush** *(Coleogyne ramosissima)*, page 61
B—Leaves longer than 1/2", not clustered; stamens fewer
. . . . Go to 5

5 A—Leaves leathery, minutely hairy on both sides; petioles less than 1/16" long . . . .
. . . . . . **Jojoba** *(Simmondsia chinensis)*, page 116
B—Leaves thin, hairless; petiole almost as long as the blade . **Singleleaf ash** *(Fraxinus anomala)*, page 124

6 A—Pistil with a single style . . . . Go to 7
B—Pistil with 2 or 3 style . . . . Go to 8

7 A—Stamens 10-45; style long, feather-like in fruit; leaf edges sharply curled under . . . .
. . . . **Mountain mahogany** *(Cercocarpus)*, page 62
B—Stamens 4 or 5; style not feathery; leaves flat, the edges not curled under . . . **Hoary coffeeberry** *(Rhamnus tomentella)*, page 64 *[Check flowers again for petals; they are present, but tiny and hard to see.]*

8 A—Sepals white to pinkish; flowers in clusters well above leafy portion of plant on thin, leafless stalks; flower clusters enclosed at the base by bracts . **Calif. buckwheat** *(Eriogonum fasciculatum)*, page 115
B—Sepals, if present, green; flowers not raised above plant on a leafless stalk . . . . Go to 9

9 A—Leaves scale-like; branches fleshy, composed of short sections connected together like beads . . . . .
. . **Iodine bush** *(Allenrolfea occidentalis)*, page 122
B—Leaves and branches not as above . . . . . Go to 10

10 A—Leaves hairless or nearly so . . . . Go to 11
B—Leaves hairy, the hairs either long and curly or short, inflated and bran-like (scurfy) . . . . . . Go to 12

11 A—Leaves roundish in cross-section, narrow, of nearly uniform width throughout; branchlets not spine-tipped
. . . . **Bush seepweed** *(Suaeda moquinii)*, page 122
B—Leaves flattened, lance-shaped; branchlets spine-tipped . . . . **Hop-sage** *(Grayia spinosa)*, page 121

12 A—Leaves densely white- or rusty-hairy; leaf edge rolled under . . . .
. . **Winter fat** *(Krascheninnikovia lanata)*, page 122
B—Leaves covered with gray or whitish inflated hairs or bran-like scales; leaf edges not rolled under . . . . .
. . . . **Saltbush** *(Atriplex)*, page 118

Key C - 4: Petals United

1 A—Corolla regular . . . .
Go to **Key C - 4.1, Petals United, Regular,** this page
B—Corolla irregular . . . .
Go to **Key C - 4.2, Petals United, Irregular,** page 31

Key C - 4.1:
Flowers
Regular

1 A—Plant spiny, the branchlets sharp-tipped or with thorns along branches . . . . Go to 2
B—Plant not spiny . . . . Go to 4

2 A—Plant a cluster of erect, cane-like, mostly unbranched stems armed with sharp thorns; leaf clusters at base of thorns during wet periods, absent during drought; flowers red, tubular, in showy clusters at branch tips
. . . . . . **Ocotillo** *(Fouquieria splendens)*, page 82
B—Plant not as above . . . . Go to 3

3 A—Branchlets bright green; calyx lobes long, thin; stamens 2; low shrub of mtns. of eastern Mojave Desert . **Greenfire** *(Menodora spinescens)*, page 123
B—Branchlets not bright green; calyx lobes more or less triangular; stamens 4-5; mid-sized shrub, widespread in both deserts . . **Desert thorn** *(Lycium)*, page 84

4 A—Leaves pinnately compound . . . .
. . . **Fairy duster** *(Calliandra eriophylla)*, page 80
B—Leaves simple . . . . Go to 5

5 A—Leaves palmately veined; a twisting tendril opposite each leaf . . . **Wild grape** *(Vitis girdiana)*, page 86
B—Leaves pinnately veined; lacking tendrils . . Go to 6

6 A—Leaves opposite or whorled . . . . Go to 7
B—Leaves alternate . . . . Go to 8

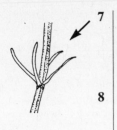

7 | A—Leaves apparently in whorls of 4–8; flowers tiny, whitish . **Bedstraw** *(Galium angustifolium)*, page 86
B—Leaves opposite; flowers purplish, large, obvious . . . . **Mtn. blue curls** *(Trichostema parishii)*, page 91

8 | A—Leaves and stems rough to the touch, with the feel of sandpaper; styles one; flowers solitary or in clusters, but not in cymes clustered at top of plant . . . . **Sandpaper plant** *(Petalonyx thurberi)*, page 80
B—Leaves not rough to the touch; styles 2; flowers in coiled or head-like cymes clustered at the top of the plant . . . . . . **Yerba santa** *(Eriodictyon)*, page 83

Key C - 4.2:
Flowers
Irregular

1 | A—Flowers scarlet, tubular, the lower lip narrow, drooping; stamens 2, the anthers just under tip of corolla's upper lip; green-stemmed, mostly leafless . . . . . . **Chuparosa** *(Justicia californica)*, page 92
B—Plant not as above . . . . Go to 2

2 | A—Leaves alternate, long and narrow (up to 5" long, usually less than 1/4" wide), sickle-shaped . . . . **Desert-willow** *(Chilopsis linearis)*, page 87
B—Leaves opposite, not as described . . . . . . Go to 3

3 | A—Corolla 2-colored, the lower lip purple, the throat and upper lip cream-colored; calyx becoming inflated into a papery, bag-like structure in fruit . . . . **Bladder sage** *(Salazaria mexicana)*, page 92
B—Corolla not 2-colored; calyx not inflated . . Go to 4

4 | A—Corolla almost regular, densely woolly, blue to purple; leaves linear, 1 1/2–3" long, mostly less than 1/8" wide . . . . **Mtn. blue curls** *(Trichostema parishii)*, page 91
B—Corolla 2-lipped, not densely woolly; leaves not as above . . . . Go to 5

5 | A—Stamens all enclosed by a sac on lower lobe of corolla; leaves with thick white hairs, especially below; plant of desert washes . . . . **Desert lavender** *(Hyptis emoryi)*, page 91
B—Stamens not enclosed by lower lip of corolla . . . . **Sage** *(Salvia)*, page 88

Key C - 5: Petals Separate

1 A—Flower irregular, petals differing in size and/or shape
.. Go to **Key C - 5.1: Flowers Irregular**, this page
B—Flower regular, all petals alike . . . . Go to 2

2 A—Leaves simple. . . . . Go to **Key C - 5.2: Flowers Regular; Leaves Simple**, page 33
B—Leaves compound . . . . Go to **Key C - 5.3: Flowers Regular; Leaves Compound**, page 34

**Key C - 5.1:
Flowers
Irregular**

1 A—Flower pea-like, an erect petal (banner) above, two petals spreading to the side (wings), two partially fused petals (keel) below enclosing the pistil and stamens; fruit an elongated pod (legume) . . Go to 2
B—Flower not as above; fruit not a pod . . . . . Go to 7

2 A—Leaves simple or lacking . . . . Go to 3
B—Leaves compound . . . . Go to 4

3 A—Leaves many; branches greenish, glandless, rarely spine-tipped. . . . . **Schott indigo bush** *(Psorothamnus schottii)*, page 76
B—Leaves mostly absent; branches gray, glandular, spine-tipped. . . . . .Smoke tree *(Psorothamnus spinosus)*, page 75

4 A—Leaves palmately compound, leaflets 5 or more . . . . **Adonis lupine** *(Lupinus excubitus)*, page 79
B—Leaves pinnately or bipinnately compound . Go to 5

5 A—Stamens not united . . . . **Rushpea** *(Caesalpinia virgata)*, page 71
B—Filaments of most or all stamens united . . . Go to 6

6 A—Flowers blue-purple (rarely rose). . . . .**Indigo bush** *(Psorothamnus)*, page 76
B—Flowers yellow, aging to red . . . . **Broom lotus** *(Lotus rigidus)*, page 79

7 A—Leaves simple; petals purplish; fruit a globose, spiny pod . . . . **Rhatany** *(Krameria)*, page 81
B—Leaves 3-foliate, ill-smelling; petals yellow; fruit an inflated bladder on a stalk . . . . **Bladderpod** *(Isomeris arborea)*, page 66

32

1 A—Leaves tiny, scale-like, closely pressed around long, thin, often drooping branchlets that resemble flexible needles *[a hand-lens may be needed to see the leaves clearly.]* . . . . **Tamarisk** *(Tamarix)*, page 70
B—Leaves not scale-like . . . . Go to 2

2 A—Leaves opposite . . . . Go to 3
B—Leaves alternate . . . . Go to 4

3 A—Leaves of two lobes fused at the base like a pair of wings; petals yellow, partially twisted; fruit a capsule with dense white or rusty hairs . . . .
. . . . . **Creosote bush** *(Larrea tridentata)*, page 58
B—Leaves simple, oval, edges often toothed; petals white, small, scoop-like; fruit a 3-lobed, sparsely haired capsule . . . .
. . **Cupleaf ceanothus** *(Ceanothus greggii)*, page 64

4 A—Leaves palmately veined . . . . Go to 5
B—Leaves pinnately veined . . . . Go to 7

5 A—Mature leaves commonly longer than 3", a twisted tendril opposite each one; stamens not joined into a tube; plant a woody vine . . . .
. . . . **Wild grape** *(Vitis girdiana)*, page 86
B—Mature leaves rarely longer than 3"; tendrils lacking; filaments of stamens joined, at least at base . Go to 6

6 A—Stamens many, the filaments forming a tube most of their length; petals red, coral or lavender, sepals green
. . **Apricot mallow** *(Sphaeralcea ambigua)*, page 63
B—Stamens 5, the filaments fused about half their length; petals missing, but large, yellow-orange sepals are often mistaken for petals *[you made this mistake, or you would not be in this key!]* . **Flannel bush** *(Fremontodendron californicum)*, page 116

7 A—Petals 4 . . . . Go to 8
B—Petals 5 . . . . Go to 9

8 A—Stamens 6, 2 shorter than the other 4 . . . .
. . . . . **Peppergrass** *(Lepidium fremontii)*, page 66
B—Stamens 8, 4 long, 4 short . . . .
Turpentine broom *(Thamnosma montana)*, page 67

9 A—Stamens 5 . . . . Go to 10
B—Stamens more than 5 . . . . Go to 13

10 A—Leaves and stems rough, having the feel of sandpaper; narrow basal parts of petals lightly joined giving appearance of a tubular corolla . . . .
. . . **Sandpaper plant** *(Petalonyx thurberi),* page 80
B—Leaves, stems not like sandpaper; petals distinct . . .
. . . . Go to 11

11 A—Stamens alternating with the petals . . . .
. . . . **Sugar bush** *(Rhus ovata),* page 68
B—Stamens opposite the petals . . . . Go to 12

12 A—Leaves in clusters (fascicles); flowers at ends of short, spur-like branchlets, solitary or clustered . . .
. . . . **Lotebush** *(Ziziphus parryi),* page 65
B—Leaves not clustered; flowers not at ends of spurs . .
Hoary coffeeberry *(Rhamnus tomentella),* page 64

13 A—Leaves divided into 3 - 7 blunt lobes, the edges rolled under, in clusters (fascicles) along the main branches
. . . . Go to 14
B—Leaves neither lobed nor rolled under; if clustered, then at the ends of short spur-like branchlets . . . .
. . . . **Desert apricot** or **almond** *(Prunus),* page 59

14 A—Flower with 1 - 5 pistils . . . . **Antelope bush**
(Purshia tridentata) or **Cliff rose** *(P. mexicana),* page 60
B—Flowers with 10 or more pistils . . . .
. . . . **Apache plume** *(Fallugia paradoxa),* page 61

Key C - 5.3:
Flowers **1** A—Leaves two-lobed, the lobes fused at base like a pair
Regular; of wings; flowers yellow, the petals partially twisted;
Leaves fruit a white- or rusty-haired capsule . . . .
Compound . . . . . **Creosote bush** *(Larrea tridentata),* page 58
B—Leaves, flowers, fruits not as above . . . . . Go to 2

2 A—Leaves with 3 leaflets . . . . Go to 3
B—Leaves with more than 3 leaflets . . . . . . Go to 4

34

3 **A**—Leaves ill-smelling, less than 2" long; fruit a swollen pod on a long stalk . . . .

. . . . . . **Bladderpod** *(Isomeris arborea)*, page 66

B—Leaves not ill-smelling, longer than 2"; fruit a berry .

. . . . **Squaw bush** *(Rhus trilobata)*, page 68

4 **A**—Older branches cherry red, swollen; a small aromatic tree or shrub of southwestern Colorado Desert . . .

. . . **Elephant tree** *(Bursera microphylla)*, page 62

B—Not as above . . . . Go to 5

5 **A**—Stamens the conspicuous part of flower, usually extending well beyond the petals; petals inconspicuous . . . . Go to 6

B—Petals the conspicuous part of flower; stamens not extending much beyond the petals . . . . . Go to 8

6 **A**—Flowers rose or reddish; stamens red, 1/2 - 3/4" long, united below into a tube; flowers in dense clusters at ends of branches . . . .

. . . **Fairy duster** *(Calliandra eriophylla)*, page 80

B—Flowers yellow; stamens not red, not so long, not united into a tube; flowers in globose heads or drooping, catkin-like spikes . . . . Go to 7

7 **A**—Stamens 10; branches with paired, straight thorns . .

. . . . **Mesquite** *(Prosopis)*, page 72

B—Stamens many; branches with curved, claw-like hooks . . . . . . **Catclaw** *(Acacia greggii)*, page 74

8 **A**—Stamens 10, but only 7 with anthers; sepals distinct

. . . . **Spiny senna** *(Senna armata)*, page 71

B—Stamens 10, all fertile; sepals fused . . . . . .Go to 9

9 **A**—Plant a large shrub or small tree with distinctly green-barked branches; spines at bases of leaves or branches spine-tipped. . . . .

. . . . **Palo verde** *(Cercidium)*, page 73

B—Plant a small, rounded shrub, less than 3' tall, its bark not green; not spinose . . . .

. . . . . . **Rushpea** *(Caesalpinia virgata)*, page 71

Key D: Shrubs not in Flower

1   **A**—Leaves small and scale-like OR plant apparently leafless . . . . Go to **Key D - 1: Scale-leaved and Leafless Shrubs,** this page
     B—Plant distinctly leafy, the leaves not tiny and scale-like . . . . Go to 2

2   **A**—Leaves thread-like (i.e., flexible, branched or not) or needle-like (ie., stiff), mostly less than 1/16" wide but occasionally to 1/8" . . . . Go to **Key D - 2: Thread- and Needle-leaved Shrubs**, page 38
     B—Leaves neither thread-like nor needle-like . . Go to 3

3   **A**—Leaves compound . . . .
     Go to **Key D - 3: Compound-leaved Shrubs**, page 42
     B—Leaves simple . . . . Go to 4

4   **A**—Leaves 12" or more long, narrow, flexible and grasslike or rigid, sharp-pointed and dagger-like, the major leaf veins running lengthwise, generally parallel to each other . . . .
     Go *back* to **Key C - 1: Shrubby Monocots**, page 24
     B—Leaves less than 12" long . . . . Go to 5

5   **A**—Leaves with 3 or more main veins arising from the base of the blade OR leaf palmately lobed . . . . . .
     Go to **Key D - 4: Palmately-veined Shrubs**, page 43
     B—Leaves with a single main vein from the base . . . .
     Go to **Key D - 5: Pinnately-veined Shrubs**, page 45

Key D - 1: Scale-leaved and Leafless Shrubs

1   **A**—Branches sharp-tipped or armed with spines or thorns . . . . Go to 2
     B—Branches not thorny or spine-tipped . . . . . Go to 8

2   **A**—Terminal branchlets sharply spine-tipped, but branches lacking spines and thorns . . . . . Go to 3
     B—Distinct spines or thorns at intervals along branches; branches themselves blunt ended . . . . . . Go to 5

3   **A**—A low, rounded shrub, to 2' tall . . . .

. . . . **Ratany** *(Krameria)*, page 81

B—A tall shrub, to 25' or more . . . . .Go to 4

4   **A**—Bark of stems ashy-gray to yellowish-green, sparsely gland-dotted; throughout the Colorado and southern Mojave Deserts . . . .

. . . . **Smoke tree** *(Psorothamnus spinosus)*, page 75

B—Bark of stems distinctly green, without glands; near Colorado River in Whipple Mtns. . . . . . . **Little-leaf palo verde** *(Cercidium microphyllum)*, page 73

5   **A**—Thorns on branches curved, clawlike . . . .

. . . . **Catclaw** *(Acacia greggii)*, page 74

B—Thorns on branches straight, not claw-like   .   Go to 6

6   **A**—Plant of several cane-like, spiny, mostly unbranched stems arising together from the ground, 6–20' tall . .

. . . . . . **Ocotillo** *(Fouquieria splendens)*, page 82

B—Plant not as above . . . . Go to 7

7   **A**—Bark green; solitary spines along stem . . . .

. . . **Blue palo verde** *(Cercidium floridum)*, page 73

B—Bark not green; spines in pairs at bases of leaves   . .

. . . . **Mesquite** *(Prosopis)*, page 72

8   **A**—Branches composed of small succulent sections linked to one another like beads on a string; stems when crushed leave dark brown stain on fingers . . .

. . **Iodine bush** *(Allenrolfea occidentalis)*, page 122

B—Branches not as above . . . . Go to 9

9   **A**—Branches and trunk thick and swollen, the bark red-brown . . . .

. . . **Elephant tree** *(Bursera microphylla)*, page 62

B—Branches not as above . . . . Go to 10

10   **A**—Leaves present, but small (less than 3/8" long) and scale-like . . . . Go to 11

B—Scale-like leaves not present . . . . Go to 15

11   **A**—Terminal branchlets slender, drooping, so tightly enclosed by tiny scale-like leaves that they resemble droopy needles . . . **Tamarisk** *(Tamarix)*, page 70

B—Terminal branchlets mostly erect or spreading, not drooping . . . . Go to 12

37

12   **A**—Leaves alternate . . . . Go to 13

      B—Leaves in pairs or triplets around the stem . Go to 14

13   **A**—All leaves scale-like . . . .

      Scale-broom *(Lepidospartum squamatum),* page 115

      B—Only the upper leaves scale-like, the lower long and narrow . . . . **Short-leaf baccharis** *(Baccharis brachyphylla),* page 110

14   **A**—Stems jointed, grooved; leaves triangular, in pairs or triplets widely spaced along an otherwise bare stem . . . . **Desert tea** *(Ephedra),* page 130

      B—Stems neither jointed nor grooved; leaf pairs or triplets closely packed so as to obscure the stem . . . . **Junipers** *(Juniperus),* page 132

15   **A**—Plant strong-scented . . . .

      Turpentine broom *(Thamnosma montana),* page 67

      B—Plant not strong-scented . . . . Go to 16

16   **A**—Stems with distinct longitudinal grooves or striations, OR with stiff, widely spaced, swollen hairs, OR with both . . . . Go to 17

      B—Stems smooth, without longitudinal grooves, striations, or stiff hairs . . . .
. . . . . . **Chuparosa** *(Justicia californica),* page 92

17   **A**—Stems with widely spaced, stiff, swollen hairs, sometimes striated; widespread in both deserts . . .
. . . . **Sweet bush** *(Bebbia juncea),* page 99

      B—Stems without stiff hairs but distinctly grooved; southern San Diego County only . . . .
Broom baccharis *(Baccharis sarothroides),* page 110

Key D -2: Thread- and Needle-leaved Shrubs

1   **A**—"Leaves" on closer inspection with a handlens really tiny and scale-like, the scales so closely packed around branchlets that branchlets resemble flexible, often drooping, needles . . . .
. . . . **Tamarisk** *(Tamarix),* page 70

      B—Leaves not scale-like . . . . Go to 2

2 A—Branches armed with thorns or spines . . . . Go to 3
B—Branches without thorns or spines . . . . . . Go to 4

3 A—"Leaves" typically 6–12" long, about 1/16" wide, flattened, ribbon-like . . . .
Mexican palo verde *(Parkinsonia aculeata)*, page 78
[Actually, what you thought were leaves are really only the rachises of compound leaves from which the tiny leaflets have already fallen.]
B—Leaves rarely exceeding 2" . . . .
. . . **Cotton-thorn** *(Tetradymia axillaris)*, page 96

4 A—Lower, older leaves lobed, the lobes long and thread-like . . . . Go to 5
B—Leaves without lobes, or the lobes not long . Go to 9

5 A—Leaves densely white-woolly below . . . . . Go to 6
B—Leaves hairless to moderately hairy below, but not woolly . . . . Go to 7

6 A—Leaf edges rolled under; leaves rarely exceeding 1 1/4", usually with fewer than 6 main lobes, the lobes rarely exceeding 1/2" in length . . . .
Golden yarrow *(Eriophyllum confertiflorum)*, page 113
B—Leaf edges not rolled under; leaves commonly reaching 3 or 4", often with 6 or more lobes, each lobe often an inch or more long . . . .
. . . **Bush groundsel** *(Senecio flaccidus)*, page 113

7 A—Leaves slightly sticky, each with a longitudinal groove on lower side tightly-packed with short hairs
. . . . **Burrobrush** *(Hymenoclea salsola)*, page 100
B—Leaves not sticky and without hair-filled groove below . . . . Go to 8

8 A—Leaves fleshy, covered with a whitish powder that rubs off; rarely with more than 2 or 3 lobes . . . . .
. . **Bush peppergrass** *(Lepidium fremontii)*, page 66
B—Leaves not fleshy, lacking white powder; commonly with 6 or more thread-like lobes . . . .
. . . **Bush groundsel** *(Senecio flaccidus)*, page 113

9 A—Leaves opposite (at least in lower part of plant) or in whorls . . . . Go to 10
B—Leaves alternate . . . . Go to 12

39

10 **A**—Leaves in whorls of 4 or more; stems squarish . . . .
. . . . . **Bedstraw** *(Galium angustifolium)*, page 86
B—Leaves opposite; stems roundish . . . . . . Go to 11

11 **A**—Leaves less than 1/2" long, in clusters (fascicles),
each leaf with 2–4 linear grooves below . . . .
. . . **Blackbush** *(Coleogyne ramosissima)*, page 61
B—Leaves to 2" long, occurring singly, without grooves;
opposite only in lower part of plant, alternate above .
. . . . **Sweet bush** *(Bebbia juncea)*, page 99

12 **A**—Leaves almost always in clusters (fascicles) along
stem, smaller leaves in axils of the larger . Go to 13
B—Leaves mostly occurring singly along stem, only
occasionally in clusters on older stems . . . Go to 17

13 **A**—Leaves dotted with small resin glands, sticky to the
touch, hairless (rarely minutely hairy). . . . .
. . . . **Goldenbush** *(Ericameria)*, page 102
B—Leaves without resin glands, hairless to densely hairy
. . . . Go to 14

14 **A**—Leaves hairless or minutely hairy; branch tips rigid,
somewhat spinose . . . .
Schott indigo bush *(Psorothamnus schottii)*, page 76
B—Leaves densely hairy; branches not spinose . Go to 15

15 **A**—Leaves sharp-pointed, sometimes spine-tipped; leaf
edges not rolled under . . . . **Little** or **Hairy**
horsebrush *(Tetradymia glabrata, T. comosa)*, page 96
B—Leaf tips blunt; leaf edges rolled under . . . Go to 16

16 **A**—Leaves pale green, usually with fine grayish hairs
(but hairless in and northeast of Joshua Tree Nat.
Monument); usually long, leafless flowering stalks
extend above leafy part of plant . . . . **Calif.**
buckwheat *(Eriogonum fasciculatum)*, page 115
B—Leaves densely white-woolly; without leafless
flowering stalks . . . .
. . **Winter fat** *(Krascheninnikovia lanata)*, page122

17 **A**—Leaves with many glands, often sticky . . . Go to 18
B—Leaves not glandular, usually not sticky . . Go to 21

18 **A**—Crushed leaves strongly odorous . . . . . Go to 19
B—Crushed leaves not strongly odorous . . . Go to 20

19 **A**—A leafy shrub, the leaves stiff, needle-like, crowded at branch tips, smelling of pine or cedar . . . .
. . **Pygmy-cedar** *(Peucephyllum schottii)*, page 101
B—A low, almost leafless shrub, the branches gland-dotted, spine-tipped . . . .
Turpentine broom *(Thamnosma montana)*, page 67

20 **A**—Leaves flattened; branches extremely thin, straight, wandlike, sometimes longitudinally grooved, much branched in upper portion; plant rarely taller than 3' .
. . . . **Matchweed** *(Gutierrezia)*, page 114
B—Leaves round in cross-section; upper branches stout, crooked, not wandlike, not grooved. . . . .
. . . . . . **Roundleaf** or **Black-stem rabbitbrush** *(Chrysothamnus teretifolius, C. paniculatus)*, page 106

21 **A**—Leaves hairless or minutely hairy . . . . . . Go to 22
B—Leaves distinctly hairy, the hairs long, obvious . . .
. . . . Go to 25

22 **A**—Leaves succulent, fleshy; a low shrub, less than 3' tall; plant of alkaline places . . . .
. . . . **Bush seepweed** *(Suaeda moquinii)*, page 123
B—Leaves not succulent, not fleshy; often taller than 3' .
. . . . Go to 23

23 **A**—Leaves often twisted; stems whitish, brittle, without ridges or grooves; a spreading shrub . . . . . **Yellow rabbitbrush** *(Chrysothamnus viscidiflorus)*, page 106
B—Leaves not twisted; stems green; an erect, broom-like shrub with grooved or ridged stems . . . . Go to 24

24 **A**—Leaves numerous, needle-like, often exceeding 1" in length; branches hairy; restricted to a few canyons on north side of San Gabriel Mtns. . . . .
Green-broom *(Lepidospartum latisquamum)*, page 115
B—Leaves sparse, to 3/4" long; branches hairless or nearly so; plants of western edge of Colorado Desert
. . . . **Broom** or **Shortleaf baccharis** *(Baccharis sarothroides, B. brachyphylla)*, page 110

25 **A**—Leaves rarely exceeding 1" in length . . . .
Gray horsebrush *(Tetradymia canescens)*, page 96
B—Leaves commonly longer than 2" . . . . . . **Rubber rabbitbrush** *(Chrysothamnus nauseosus)*, page 106

Key D - 3: Compound-leaved Shrubs

1   **A**—Each leaf composed of two wing-like leaflets attached together at the base . . . .
. . . . . **Creosote bush** *(Larrea tridentata)*, page 58
B—Leaf not as above . . . . Go to 2

2   **A**—Leaves trifoliate, with three (occasionally 5) simple leaflets . . . . Go to 3
B—Leaves not as above . . . . Go to 5

3   **A**—Leaflets lobed . . . .
. . . . **Squaw bush** *(Rhus trilobata)*, page 68
B—Leaflets smooth-edged . . . . Go to 4

4   **A**—Crushed foliage foul-smelling . . . .
. . . . . . **Bladderpod** *(Isomeris arborea)*, page 66
B—Foliage not foul-smelling . . . .
. . . . **Broom lotus** *(Lotus rigidus)*, page 79

5   **A**—Leaves palmately compound . . . .
. . . . . **Adonis lupine** *(Lupinus excubitus)*, page 79
B—Leaves pinnately compound . . . . Go to 6

6   **A**—Leaves once pinnately compound . . . . . . Go to 7
B—Leaves at least twice pinnately compound *[Check several leaves; petioles are often so short that the two leaflets, each bearing many pinnules, appear to arise separately from the stem.]* . . . . . . Go to 11

7   **A**—Leaflets tiny, alternating along a flattened, green rachis that may reach 12" in length and persists after leaflets have fallen; spines in 3s, reddish; bark of branches green . . . .
Mexican palo verde *(Parkinsonia aculeata)*, page 78
B—Leaflets opposite each other; rachis not flattened; spines (if present) not in threes . . . . Go to 8

8   **A**—Leaves with an even number of leaflets, that is, all leaflets paired, there being no unpaired leaflet at the tip . . . . Go to 9
B—Leaflets odd numbered, an unpaired leaflet at the tip
. . . . Go to 10

9   **A**—Leaves with 4 or fewer pairs of widely spaced leaflets; plant a small shrub, to 2' tall . . . .
. . . . **Spiny senna** *(Senna armata)*, page 71
B—Leaves with 4 or more pairs of leaflets; a small tree, to 35' tall . . . **Ironwood** *(Olneya tesota)*, page 77

10 **A**—Leaves 1–2" long; leaflets 7–35; strongly aromatic .
. . . **Elephant tree** *(Bursera microphylla)*, page 62
B—Leaves 1/2 to 1 1/2" long; leaflets mostly 3–7 (up to 17 in one species); not strongly aromatic . . . . . .
. . . . **Indigo bush** *(Psorothamnus)*, page 76

11 **A**—Bark of branches bright green . . . .
. . . . **Palo verde** *(Cercidium)*, page 73
B—Bark of branches not green . . . . Go to 12

12 **A**—Branches with stout thorns or spines . . . Go to 13
B—Branches thornless . . . . Go to 14

13 **A**—Thorns single, curved, clawlike . . . .
. . . . **Catclaw** *(Acacia greggii)*, page 74
B—Thorns usually paired, straight . . . .
. . . . **Mesquite** *(Prosopis)*, page 72

14 **A**—Leaves with 3 pinnae; terminal pinna with 5–13 pairs of pinnules, lateral pinnae with 4–9 pairs . . . . . .
. . . . . . **Rushpea** *(Caesalpinia virgata)*, page 71
B—Leaves with 2–4 pairs of pinnae, each with 5–12 pairs of pinnules . . . .
. . . **Fairy duster** *(Calliandra eriophylla)*, page 80

Key D - 4: Palmately-veined Shrubs

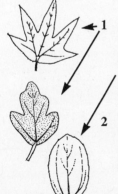

1   **A**—Leaf with 5 or more prominent veins from the base OR the blade with lobes arranged in a distinct palmate pattern OR both . . . . Go to 2
B—Leaf with only 3 prominent veins from the base, the blade not distinctly palmately lobed . . . . Go to 6

2   **A**—Mature leaves large, the blades 4" or more across . .
. . . . Go to 3
B—Mature leaves small, the blades less than 4" across .
. . . . Go to 4

43

3 **A**—A twisted tendril opposite each leaf; plant a vine . .
. . . . **Wild grape** *(Vitis girdiana)*, page 86
B—Tendrils lacking; not a vine. . . . .
. . . . . **Castor bean** *(Ricinus communis)*, page 117

4 **A**—Branches flexible, little-branched; leaves arising singly along main branches . . . .
. . **Apricot mallow** *(Sphaeralcea ambigua)*, page 63
B—Branches rigid, much-branched; leaves usually in clusters on the tips of short, spur-like branches . . .
. . . . Go to 5

5 **A**—Mature leaves 1/2" or less long, deeply cleft into 3 (occasionally 5) narrow lobes, sticky. . . . .
. . . . **Antelope bush** *(Purshia tridentata)*, page 60
B—Mature leaves longer, not deeply cleft, covered with rusty-colored, star-shaped hairs . . . . **Flannel bush** *(Fremontodendron californicum)*, page 116

6 **A**—Leaves opposite . . . .
. . . **Desert sunflower** *(Viguiera parishii)*, page 100
B—Leaves alternate . . . . Go to 7

7 **A**—Leaves strongly aromatic, widest at the tip and ending in 3 (sometimes 5 or 7) finger-like lobes . . .
. . . . **Sagebrush** *(Artemisia)*, page 104
B—Leaf not aromatic, not as described . . . . . Go to 8

8 **A**—Leaves hairless, often sticky . . . . Go to 9
B—Leaves hairy, at least when young . . . . . Go to 10

9 **A**—Leaf edges distinctly lobed or toothed . . . .
. . . . **Emory baccharis** *(Baccharis emoryi)* or **Mule fat** *(B. salicifolia)*, page 110
B—Leaf edges smooth . . . .
. **Inyo brickellbush** *(Brickellia multiflora)*, page 108

10 **A**—Leaf edges, especially of older leaves, toothed or lobed . . . . **White** or **Calif. brickell-bush** *(Brickellia incana, B. californica)*, page 108
B—Leaf edges smooth . . . .
. . . . . **Brittlebush** or **Encelia** *(Encelia)*, page 94

Key D - 5: Pinnately-veined Shrubs

1 A—Leaves opposite or whorled . . . .
   . . . Go to **Key D - 5.1: Leaves Opposite**, this page
   B—Leaves alternate . . . . Go to 2

2 A—Edges of leaves smooth, without lobes, teeth, or
   notches . . . . Go to **Key
   D - 5.2: Leaves Alternate, Smooth-edged**, page 46
   B—Edges of leaves variously toothed, lobed, or notched
   . . . . Go to **Key
   D - 5.3: Leaves Alternate, Toothed or Lobed**, page 49

Key D - 5.1:

Leaves   1 A—Leaves in whorls of 4 or more . . . .
Opposite   . . . . . **Bedstraw** *(Galium angustifolium)*, page 86
           B—Leaves in pairs opposite each other . . . . . Go to 2

2 A—Each leaf composed of two wing-like leaflets
   attached at the base . . . .
   . . . . . **Creosote bush** *(Larrea tridentata)*, page 58
   B—Each leaf not as above . . . . Go to 3

3 A—Branchlets nearly square in cross-section **OR** leaves
   aromatic when crushed **OR** both . . . . Go to 4
   B—Branchlets not squarish; leaves not aromatic . Go to 8

4 A—Plant tree-like, with a distinct trunk; leaves not
   aromatic, usually simple, the blade round or oval,
   but occasionally compound with three leaflets; plant
   of mountains of eastern Mojave desert . . . .
   . . . . **Singleleaf ash** *(Fraxinus anomala)*, page 124
   B—Plant shrubby; leaves always simple, usually
   aromatic . . . . Go to 5

5 A—Leaves long (up to 2") and narrow, densely woolly
   below, in clusters along stem . . . .
   Mountain blue curls *(Trichostema parishii)*, page 91
   B—Leaves not as above . . . . Go to 6

6 A—Leaf blade broadest at base, covered with white hairs
   . . . . . . **Desert lavender** *(Hyptis emoryi)*, page 91
   B—Leaf blade broadest near middle and, at best, slightly
   hairy . . . . Go to 7

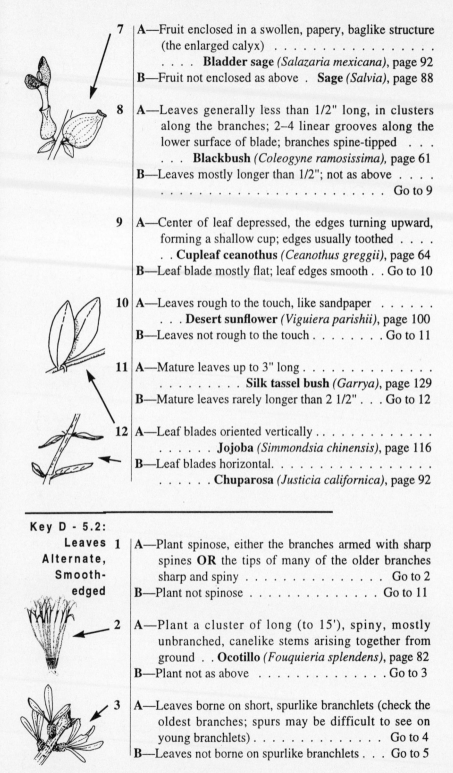

7 A—Fruit enclosed in a swollen, papery, baglike structure (the enlarged calyx) . . . .
. . . . **Bladder sage** *(Salazaria mexicana)*, page 92
B—Fruit not enclosed as above . **Sage** *(Salvia)*, page 88

8 A—Leaves generally less than 1/2" long, in clusters along the branches; 2–4 linear grooves along the lower surface of blade; branches spine-tipped . . .
. . . **Blackbush** *(Coleogyne ramosissima)*, page 61
B—Leaves mostly longer than 1/2"; not as above . . . .
. . . . Go to 9

9 A—Center of leaf depressed, the edges turning upward, forming a shallow cup; edges usually toothed . . . .
. . **Cupleaf ceanothus** *(Ceanothus greggii)*, page 64
B—Leaf blade mostly flat; leaf edges smooth . . Go to 10

10 A—Leaves rough to the touch, like sandpaper . . . . . .
. . . **Desert sunflower** *(Viguiera parishii)*, page 100
B—Leaves not rough to the touch . . . . Go to 11

11 A—Mature leaves up to 3" long . . . .
. . . . **Silk tassel bush** *(Garrya)*, page 129
B—Mature leaves rarely longer than 2 1/2" . . . Go to 12

12 A—Leaf blades oriented vertically . . . .
. . . . . . **Jojoba** *(Simmondsia chinensis)*, page 116
B—Leaf blades horizontal. . . . .
. . . . . . **Chuparosa** *(Justicia californica)*, page 92

Key D - 5.2:
Leaves
Alternate,
Smooth-
edged

1 A—Plant spinose, either the branches armed with sharp spines **OR** the tips of many of the older branches sharp and spiny . . . . Go to 2
B—Plant not spinose . . . . Go to 11

2 A—Plant a cluster of long (to 15'), spiny, mostly unbranched, canelike stems arising together from ground . . **Ocotillo** *(Fouquieria splendens)*, page 82
B—Plant not as above . . . . Go to 3

3 A—Leaves borne on short, spurlike branchlets (check the oldest branches; spurs may be difficult to see on young branchlets) . . . . Go to 4
B—Leaves not borne on spurlike branchlets . . . Go to 5

4 **A**—Leaves narrow, rarely exceeding 1/4" in width, broadest near the tip . . . .
. . . . **Desert almond** *(Prunus fasciculata)*, page 59
B—Leaves oval, commonly 1/4–1/2" in width, broadest at or below the middle . . . .
. . . . **Lotebush** *(Ziziphus parryi)*, page 65

5 **A**—Young stems covered with a dense mat of woolly hairs . . . . Go to 6
B—Young stems without dense wool . . . . . . Go to 7

6 **A**—Leaves in clusters; fruit a hairy achene . . . .
Cotton-thorn, Mojave or **Hairy horsebrush** *(Tetradymia axillaris, T. stenolepis, T. comosa)*, page 96
B—Leaves occurring singly; fruit a spiny, globular pod .
. . . . **Rhatany** *(Krameria)*, page 81

7 **A**—Leaves scurfy, that is, covered with small, gray or white, inflated, bran-like hairs . . . . Go to 8
B—Leaves not scurfy . . . . Go to 9

8 **A**—Leaves distinctly fleshy . . . .
. . . . **Hop-sage** *(Grayia spinosa)*, page 121
B—Leaves not fleshy, or only slightly so . . . .
. . . . **Parry saltbush, Spinescale, Shadscale** *(Atriplex parryi, A. spinifera, A. confertifolia)*, page 118

9 **A**—Plant nearly leafless, its few leaves scattered, solitary, non-fleshy; bark gray-green, dotted with brownish glands . . . .
. . . **Smoke tree** *(Psorothamnus spinosus)*, page 75
B—Plant with many leaves, either solitary or in clusters, often fleshy; bark not glandular . . . . . . Go to 10

10 **A**—Leaves in clusters; stems not bright green . . . . . .
. . . . **Desert thorn** *(Lycium)*, page 84
B—Leaves mostly solitary; stems bright green . . . . . .
. . . . **Greenfire** *(Menodora spinescens)*, page 123

11 **A**—Leaves distinctly scurfy, that is, covered with small, gray or white, inflated, bran-like hairs . . **Fourwing saltbush, Big saltbush** or **Allscale** *(Atriplex canescens, A. lentiformis, A. polycarpa)*, page 118
B—Leaves not scurfy . . . . Go to 12

12 A—Leaves less than 3 times longer than wide . Go to 13
B—Leaves 3 or more times longer than wide . . Go to 19

13 A—Twigs distinctly reddish . . . . Go to 14
B—Twigs not reddish . . . . Go to 15

14 A—Leaf blade folded upwards at the midrib so that leaves take the shape of a taco shell . . . .
. . . . **Sugar bush** *(Rhus ovata)*, page 68
B—Leaf blade flat . . . .
. **Hoary coffeeberry** *(Rhamnus tomentella)*, page 64

15 A—Blade attached directly to the stem, the petiole lacking (or nearly so) . . . . Go to 16
B—Leaves with a distinct petiole . . . . Go to 18

16 A—Leaves covered with stiff hairs, very rough (sandpapery) to the touch . . . .
. . . **Sandpaper plant** *(Petalonyx thurberi)*, page 81
B—Leaves not as above . . . . Go to 17

17 A—Plant broomlike, often nearly leafless; leaves hairless .
Squaw waterweed *(Baccharis sergiloides)*, page110
B—Plant leafy, not broomlike; leaves soft, white-hairy .
. **White brickellbush** *(Brickellia incana)*, page 108

18 A—Blade nearly circular on a broad petiole (like a ping-pong paddle), hairless, dotted with tiny depressed glands . . . .
Wedgeleaf goldenbush *(Ericameria cuneata)*, page 102
B—Leaf blade longer than wide, hairy, not glandular . .
. . . . **Brittlebush, Encelia** *(Encelia)*, page 94

19 A—Leaves commonly 2" or more long . . . . . Go to 20
B—Leaves rarely exceeding 1 1/2" in length . . Go to 21

20 A—Leaves mostly 2 to 4" long, often exceeding 1/2" in width . . . . **Goodding's or Arroyo willow** *(Salix gooddingii, S. lasiolepis)*, page 126
B—Leaves to 6" long, of nearly uniform width throughout (less than 1/4") . . . .
. . . . . **Desert-willow** *(Chilopsis linearis)*, page 87

21 A—Leaves in clusters; leaf edges rolled under . Go to 22
B—Leaves borne singly; leaf edges not rolled under . . .
. . . . Go to 23

22 A—Leaf clusters at tips of short, stout, spur-like branchlets; leaves thick and leathery, the midrib prominent; an erect shrub to 10' tall . . . . **Mountain mahogany** *(Cercocarpus)*, page 62

B—Leaf clusters arise from sides of stems; leaves flexible, the midrib not particularly prominent; a low spreading shrub to 3' tall . . . . **Calif. buckwheat** *(Eriogonum fasciculatum)*, page 115

23 A—A 3 - 9' tall shrub; stems erect, straight, mostly unbranched, willow-like . . . . **Arrowweed** *(Pluchea sericea)*, page 112

B—Plant rarely taller than 2'; stems not as above . . . . Go to 24

24 A—Leaves hairless; plant sparsely leafy . . . . **Goldenhead** *(Acamptopappus)*, page 98

B—Leaves hairy; plant distinctly leafy . . . . . Go to 25

25 A—Leaves distinctly hairy, the hairs either short and white or long, soft and kinky; leaves often dotted with depressed glands . . . . **Mojave** or **Rigid brickellbush** *(Brickellia oblongifolia, B. frutescens)*, page 108

B—Leaves minutely hairy; lacking depressed glands . . . . . . **California trixis** *(Trixis californica)*, page 99

Key D - 5.3: Leaves Alternate, Toothed or Lobed

1 A—Petiole several times longer than blade . . . . **Arrowleaf** *(Pleurocoronis pluriseta)*, page 112

B—Petiole shorter than blade or lacking . . . . . Go to 2

2 A—Leaves strongly aromatic when crushed . . . Go to 3

B—Leaves lacking strong odor when crushed . Go to 4

3 A—Leaves typically broadest at or near the tip and ending in 3 (sometimes 5 or 7) tooth- or finger-like lobes . . . . **Sagebrush** *(Artemisia)*, page 104

B—Leaves widest near the middle, lacking lobes at tip . . . . **Yerba santa** *(Eriodictyon)*, page 83

4 A—Leaves in tight clusters (fascicles), divided near the tip into 3 to 7 lobes, the edges rolled under . Go to 5

B—Leaves not clustered, not divided at the tip into 3 to 7 lobes, the edges not rolled under . . . . . . Go to 6

5 | A—Leaves 1/2 - 1" long, 3-7 lobed . . . .
. . . . . **Apache plume** *(Fallugia paradoxa)*, page 61
B—Leaves less than 1/2" long, mostly 3 (occasionally 5) lobed . . . . **Antelope bush** *(Purshia tridentata)* or **Cliff rose** *(P. mexicana)*, page 60

6 | A—Leaves less than 1" long, divided into many small rounded lobes; leaves and stems densely covered with stiff white hairs; a low (1-2' high) rounded bush with white stems . . . .
. . . . . . **Burro-weed** *(Ambrosia dumosa)*, page 93
B—Not as above. . . . . Go to 7

7 | A—Leaves rough to the touch, sandpapery . . . .
. . . **Sandpaper plant** *(Petalonyx thurberi)*, page 81
B—Leaves not rough to the touch . . . . Go to 8

8 | A—Leaf blade 3 or more times as long as wide . Go to 9
B—Blade less than 3 times as long as wide . . . Go to 12

9 | A—Older leaves mostly 3-veined, the two outer veins less prominent than the central . **Mule fat** *(Baccharis salicifolia)* or **Emory baccharis** *(B. emoryi)*, page 110
B—Older leaves not 3-veined . . . . Go to 10

10 | A—Leaves long and narrow, up to 5" long and 3/8" wide; leaf edges finely toothed . . . .
. . . **Narrow-leaved willow** *(Salix exigua)*, page 126
B—Leaf edge shorter and broader, irregular lobed . . .
. . . . Go to 11

11 | A—Blade with depressed glands; all lobes of leaf about equal in length and shorter than the width of the main axis; older stems hairless, white, shining; plant of western edge of both deserts . . . .
Pale-leaf goldenbush *(Isocoma acradenia)*, page 103
B—Leaf glandless; lobes of varying length, the lower often longer than the width of main leaf axis; older stems with dense mat of short, white hairs; plant of mountains of eastern Mojave Desert . . . .
. . **Woolly bursage** *(Ambrosia eriocentra)*, page 93

12 | A—Young twigs distinctly reddish . . . . Go to 13
B—Young twigs not reddish . . . . Go to 15

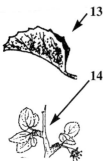

13 A—Leaf blade folded upward at midrib like a taco shell .
. . . . **Sugar bush** *(Rhus ovata)*, page 68
B—Leaf blade flat . . . . Go to 14

14 A—Leaves borne on short spurlike branchlets; leaves
often almost as wide as long. . . . .
. . . . . **Desert apricot** *(Prunus fremontii)*, page 59
B—Leaves not on spurlike branchlets; leaves mostly
about twice as long as wide . . . .
Hoary coffeeberry *(Rhamnus tomentella)*, page 64

15 A—Leaves typically edged with several pointed,
sometimes sharp, spines or teeth; if leaf smooth-
edged or round-lobed then fruit an acorn (Muller's
oak) . . . . Go to 16
B—Leaf edges without sharp spines or teeth . . **Pungent,
Desert,** or **Littleleaf brickellbush** *(Brickellia
arguta, B. desertorum, B. microphylla)*, page 108

16 A—A small shrub, rarely exceeding 3' in height; leaf
blade undulating and wavy, not flat, and covered
with bran-like scales (scurfy); fruit not an acorn . .
. . . **Desert holly** *(Atriplex hymenelytra)*, page 118
B—A large, stout shrub, to 15' tall; leaf blade more or
less flattened, either hairless or with star-shaped
hairs; fruit an acorn . . . .
. . . . **Desert oaks** *(Quercus)*, page 128

Notes

California fan palm *(Washingtonia filifera)*

Palm Family (Phoenicaceae)
ARECAECAE

Distribution: Clustered around seeps, springs, watercourses, usually below 3500'; CBS.

Description: A tall (to 55'), columnar tree with an unbranched trunk and a cluster of large, fan-like leaves at its apex. Leaf blades 3-6' long, plaited like an accordion; petioles thick, as long as blades, armed with stout, sharp, hooked spines. Lvs. drooping and forming a thatch around trunk as they die (unless removed by fire or pruning). Flrs. white, in a tight spike (spadix) projecting from a leaflike bract (spathe); inflorescence, including peduncle, may reach 12' in length. Fr. a black-skinned drupe.

Notes: From these plants, sure indicators of freshwater, have come the names of several southern California towns: Palm Springs, Twenty-nine Palms, Palm Desert, Thousand Palms. They have been planted extensively in cities throughout the southwest. Our species is of little economic importance, but other palms have found use by humans as a source of coconuts, dates, palm oil, palm hearts, waxes, even building materials.

Related species: California fan palm is the only palm native to California. The **Date palm**, *Phoenix dactilifera*, is grown commercially in many desert regions, however. Aside from the fact that it typically grows in groves, date palm can be distinguished by its long, feather-like leaves, distinctly different in form from the fan-shaped leaves of *W. filifera*.

53

Joshua tree *(Yucca brevifolia)*

Agave Family (Agavaceae)

Distribution: Dry mesas and slopes, 2000-6000'; JTW. Southern limit of this species in Joshua Tree National Monument marks the southern boundary of the Mojave Desert.

Description: A tree (occasionally shrub-like), to 30' tall, unbranched when young, branched to form an open crown when older. Lvs. dagger-like, sharp-pointed, usually less than 12" long, in tufts at tips of branches; leaf edges finely toothed, lacking fibers. Flrs. in panicles up to 14" long at branch tips. Perianth greenish-white, its segments 1 - 1 1/2" long, fleshy, waxy. St. 6, shorter than perianth; Ov. sup., 3-celled. Fr. a dry, ovoid capsule, 2-4" long. April - May.

Notes: Joshua tree is a dominant plant over much of the Mojave Desert, sometimes forming extensive woodlands. As with other yuccas, reproduction depends upon a moth *(genus Pronuba)* that gathers pollen from flowers, places it on a stigma thereby fertilizing it, then lays its eggs on the fertilized flower. The moth's larvae eat some seeds, but the tree cannot set seeds at all without the moth's help. This is a classic example of mutualism, an interdependency between two species so tight that neither can survive alone.

Desert-dwelling Indians ground the seeds of the Joshua Tree into a flour that was eaten either dry or in a mush. The red roots of the tree provided the red strands used in many Indian baskets. The light, strong wood of the trees was used briefly during war-time for making splints.

The Joshua Tree provides a habitat critical for the survival of many animals. Pack rats commonly build nests in piles of debris at the base of Joshua trees. The yucca night lizard, *Xantusia vigilis*, lives only in and under these plants. Many birds, such as flickers, woodpeckers, wrens, flycatchers, and titmice, nest in the tree's branches or in holes in their trunks. Thus, the destruction of vast numbers of these plants for housing tracts dooms many of these animals.

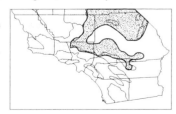

Desert yuccas *(Yucca)*

Agave Family (Agavaceae)

Key to species:

1 | **A**—Edges of leaves with coarse, peeling fibers . . . . Go to 3
      | **B**—Edges of leaves minutely sawtoothed, lacking coarse fibers . . . Go to 2

2 | **A**—Trunkless; plant a rosette of leaves directly on ground; leaves 2–3' long; on desert-facing mountain slopes. . . . **Chaparral yucca** *(Y. whipplei)*
      | **B**—Trunk present; leaf rosettes on tip of trunk or branches; leaves scarcely 12" long; Mojave Des. . **Joshua tree** *(Yucca brevifolia)*, preceding page

3 | **A**—Plant to 12' tall, usually with a distinct, often branched, trunk; flowering stalk less than 2' tall; rocky slopes and mesas below about 5000' . . . . **Mojave yucca** *(Y. schidigera)*
      | **B**—Plant to 3' tall, trunkless, growing on ground; flowering stalk 3–4' long; Mtns. of eastern Mojave Desert . . . . **Banana yucca** *(Y. baccata)*

Distribution: Mojave yucca; CBS, Cha. Banana yucca; JTW. Chaparral yucca; Cha, JTW.

Description: Leaves sharp-pointed, dagger-like. Flrs. cream-colored to purplish, the perianth (sepals + petals) segments fused to mid-point. Fr. a fleshy capsule. March–June.

Notes: Indians made extensive use of all yuccas. The leaves provided fibers for rope, sandals and cloth. Young flowers, though bitter, were eaten. Fruits with the skin removed were consumed raw, roasted, or pounded into a meal. The large, black seeds were roasted and eaten whole or ground into a flour. Roots pounded in water produce a lather that served as a soap, called "amole," used in ritual washings and as a shampoo.

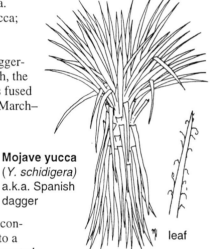

Mojave yucca
(Y. schidigera)
a.k.a. Spanish dagger

leaf

Mojave yucca

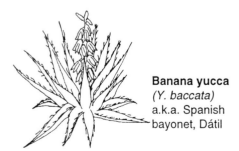

Banana yucca
(Y. baccata)
a.k.a. Spanish bayonet, Dátil

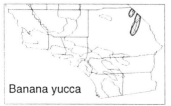

Banana yucca

Nolina *(Nolina)*

Agave Family (Agavaceae)

Key to species:

1 |A—Leaves concave, narrow (3/8 - 5/8") just above the expanded base; plant of Joshua tree or pinyon-juniper woodlands in the Santa Rosa and San Jacinto Mtns. or of chaparral of San Diego, Orange and Riverside Cos. . . . . **Parry nolina** *(N. parryi)*

B—Leaves flat, 5/8 - 1 1/4" wide just above the expanded base . . . Go to 2

2 |A—Leaf edges smooth except for shredding brown fibers; perianth less than 1/8" in length; sporadic in creosote bush scrub below 3000' on mtns. bordering Colorado Desert . . . . **Bigelow nolina** *(N. bigelovii)*

B—Leaf edges finely sawtoothed, rough to the touch, with stiff, bristly hairs; perianth almost 1/4" long; plant of Joshua tree and pinyon-juniper woodlands on high desert slopes (3500-6500') of San Jacinto Mtns. and in Little San Bernardino, Kingston and Eagle Mtns. . **Wolf nolina** *(N. wolfii)*

Description: Nolinas are yucca-like plants, usually with short, thick, unbranched, woody trunks. The long (2-4'), narrow, grasslike leaves are clustered at the trunk's apex, or if a trunk is lacking, on the soil surface. In Parry and Bigelow nolina the trunk typically is 1-3' tall; the trunk of Wolf nolina often exceeds 6' in height. Flrs. white or creamy, borne in a showy cluster on a leafless stalk arising from the trunk apex. Perianth segments 6, separate; St. 6, with very short filaments, aborted in fertile flowers; Ov. sup., deeply 3-lobed.

Parry nolina
(N. parryi)

Related species: A fourth species, *N. interrata,* is apparently restricted to a small region 8 miles east of El Cajon, San Diego Co. It is readily recognized by its habit of growing from an underground stem, hence has leaf clusters emerging at ground level.

Notes: Livestock sometimes graze the leaves in times of drought but sheep are poisoned by eating them.

Bigelow nolina

Century plant *(Agave deserti)*

a.k.a. Maguey, Mescal, Desert agave   Agave Family (Agavaceae)

Distribution: Dry rocky slopes and washes, 1500 - 5000'; CBS, ShS.

Description: A rosette of leaves growing directly on the ground. Lvs. thick, fleshy, 6 -16" long, sharp spines along edges and at tips. Flowers at maturity, a 6 - 15' tall flr. stalk growing from center of rosette. Flrs. many, yellow, 1 1/2 - 2" long, in groups on branches of flowering stalk. Perianth of 6 segments, funnel-shaped; St. 6, at top of perianth, extending beyond; Ov. inf., 3-celled. Fr. a 1 1/2 - 2 1/2" long, dry, oblong capsule. After flowering, plant dies. May - July.

Notes: The erroneous belief that this plant lives 100 years before flowering and dying provides its name. In fact, most flower after 20 - 40 years. The plants also reproduce vegetatively so that dying plants often leave a ring of young progeny around them.

Fibers of the leaves were used by desert-dwelling Indians in the manufacture of rope, bowstrings and cloth. Spines on leaf tips served as needles. Young flower stalks and the heart of the plant were eaten after being roasted in a pit for up to 3 days; excess was dried and used for bartering with other tribes. Roasted, boiled or dried young buds were also consumed and seeds were sometimes ground into flour and eaten as a gruel. Some tribes, notably the Apaches of Arizona, produced an alcoholic drink from the juices of this and other agaves.

Related agaves are cultivated in Mexico and Central America for their fibers, known in commerce as sisal or henequen. Other agaves are the source of popular alcoholic beverages. The fermented juices produce "pulque;" tequila and mescal are distilled from pulque.

leaf

Related species: *A. utahensis,* also called century plant, is found on limestone slopes of the mountains of the eastern Mojave Desert. Its leaves are shorter (4-10'), its flower clusters smaller (4 or fewer).

Creosote bush *(Larrea tridentata)*

Caltrops Family (Zygophyllaceae)

Distribution: Mesas and plains of the Mojave and Colorado Deserts below 5000'; CBS.

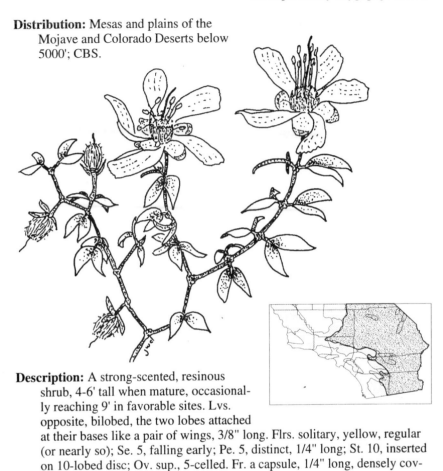

Description: A strong-scented, resinous shrub, 4-6' tall when mature, occasionally reaching 9' in favorable sites. Lvs. opposite, bilobed, the two lobes attached at their bases like a pair of wings, 3/8" long. Flrs. solitary, yellow, regular (or nearly so); Se. 5, falling early; Pe. 5, distinct, 1/4" long; St. 10, inserted on 10-lobed disc; Ov. sup., 5-celled. Fr. a capsule, 1/4" long, densely covered with whitish hairs. Nov. - May.

Notes: Creosote is undoubtedly the most common desert shrub of California. Almost pure stands occur in many parts of our deserts. The shrubs are long-lived; some are remnants (clones) of plants established more than 11,000 yrs. ago.

Indians used a decoction of leaves as an antiseptic on sores and wounds and bathed in it as an aid for rheumatism. A tea made from the leaves was drunk both as an emetic and as treatment for upset stomachs, colds, tuberculosis and venereal diseases (though its efficacy as a treatment is highly questionable!). Its resins provided a glue used in arrowmaking and pottery mending. In Mexico, flower buds are eaten pickled in vinegar. Today, a chemical from the plant finds its way into many food products as a fat preservative.

Desert almond, Desert apricot *(Prunus)*

Rose Family (Rosaceae)

Key to species:

1 | **A**—Leaves narrow, less than 1/2" long, smooth-edged (rarely 1- or 2-toothed), with almost no petiole; flowers stalkless; fruit densely covered with brown bristly hairs, the stone smooth; dry slopes and washes of Mojave Desert and northern and western borders of Colorado Desert, 2500 to 6000' . . . . **Desert almond** *(P. fasciculata)*

B—Leaves oval or roundish, to 3/4" long, about as wide, edges finely saw-toothed, the petiole up to 1/2" long; flowers on stalks to 1/2" long; fruit yellowish with tiny downy hairs, the stone ridged below; slopes of arid canyons below 4000' on the Colorado Desert's western edge . . . .
. . . . **Desert apricot** *(P. fremontii)*

Distribution: Desert apricot; CBS, PJW.
Desert almond; CBS, JTW, PJW.

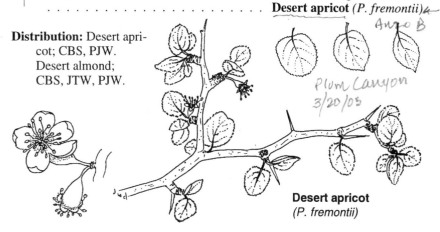

Anjo B

Plum Canyon
3/20/05

Desert apricot
(P. fremontii)

Description: Much-branched, deciduous shrubs, 2 - 6' (D. apricot) or up to 15' (D. almond) tall. Branchlets short, stiff somewhat sharp-tipped. Lvs. on stubby, spurlike branchlets, tightly clustered (fascicled) in D. almond. Flrs. solitary or 2-3 together. Se. 5, united at base with receptacle; Pe. 5, white, separate; St. many; Ov. sup., 1-celled. Fr. a dry drupe. March-May (D. almond), Feb.- April (D. apricot).

Related species: Desert peach *(P. andersonii)* barely reaches so. California on the dry desert slopes of Kern Co. It is more typical of the Sierra Nevadas from Inyo Co. northward.

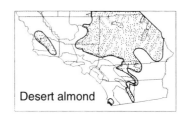

Desert almond

Desert almond
(P. fasciculata)

Antelope bush, Cliff rose *(Purshia)*

Rose Family (Rosaceae)

Key to species:

1 | **A**—Leaves to 3/8" long, deeply cleft into 3 (rarely 5) linear lobes; pistil 1; stamens 20-30, in a single row; fruit hairy, swollen at base, the style persisting as a curved neck (to 1/2"); from 2800-9000' in Mojave and w. Colorado Desert and along transverse ranges to Mt. Pinos . . . .
. . . . **Antelope bush** *(P. tridentata)*
B—Leaves to 5/8" long, divided pinnately into 5-9 narrow lobes; pistils mostly 4 or 5 (occasionally more); stamens many, in two rows; fruit an achene with a feathery tail to 2" long; 3500-8000' in Clark, New York, Providence Mtns. of eastern Mojave Desert . . **Cliff rose** *(P. mexicana)*

Distribution: Antelope bush: Desert cyns., dry mtn. slopes; Cha, JTW, PJW. Cliff rose: Limestone hills; JTW, PJW.

Cliff rose

Description: A shrub, either erect, 2-8' tall (Antelope bush) or scraggly, 1-6' tall (Cliff rose). Lvs. alt., the edges rolled under, crowded at ends of twigs, the blade gland-dotted, sticky. Flrs. solitary on short, lateral branches (Antelope bush) or showy, 1/2-3/4" across, on glandular stalks up to 1/2" long at ends of short branchlets (Cliff rose). Se. 5, fused to receptacle; Pe. 5, separate, white or pale yellow; Ov. sup. 1-celled. April-June (Cliff rose) or July (Antelope bush).

MdW

Cliff Rose
(P. mexicana)
a.k.a. Quinine bush

Notes: Foliage has a bitter taste to humans, but both plants are heavily browsed by game and livestock. Indians used the shredding bark of Cliff rose to make clothing, mats and sandals. Steeping the leaves of Cliff rose gently makes a refreshing tea; if strong, the tea acts as an emetic.

Antelope bush
(P. tridentata)
a.k.a. Waxy bitterbrush

MdW

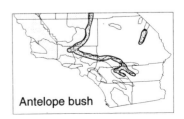

Antelope bush

Apache plume *(Fallugia paradoxa)*

Rose Family (Rosaceae)

Distribution: Rocky slopes, 3500-7000'; JTW, PJW.

Description: A sparsely-branched bush, 1-6' tall, with flaky, straw-colored bark. Lvs. alt., 1/2-1" long, with 3-7 blunt lobes, their edges rolled under, green above, rusty-woolly beneath, in clusters along branches. Flrs. 1- 1 1/2" across, alone on leafless stalks: Se. 5, alternating with 5 small bracts; Pe. 5, white; St. many, in 3 ranks; Pi. many, hairy; Ov. sup., 1-celled. Fr. an achene with long, reddish, feathery tail. April-May.

Notes: Livestock and deer eat this plant. Indians of northern Arizona used a decoction from the leaves to promote hair growth. Joint pain was treated with a powder made from the roots mixed with similar powders from the tobacco plant or horehound *(Marubium vulgare)*. Boiled, the roots provided a tonic used to treat coughs, the leaves for indigestion.

MdW

Blackbush *(Coleogyne ramosissima)*

a.k.a. Blackbrush

Rose Family (Rosaceae)

Distribution: Dry slopes, 2000-5000'; CBS, JTW. Common in e. Mojave Desert, occasional in w. Colorado Desert.

Description: A low (1-6' tall), shrub with spine-tipped branches. Ashy-gray bark turns black with age. Lvs. thick, linear or club-shaped, 1/4-1/2" long, in opposite clusters; blade flat above, with 2-4 linear grooves below, the edge smooth, somewhat rolled under; short petiole remains on stem after lvs. fall. Flrs. solitary, 1/4-1/2" across, at ends of short branchlets, with 2 to 4 3-lobed bracts beneath. Se. 4, petal-like, yellowish, united at base; Pe. none; St. 20 to 40; Ov. sup., 1-celled, sheathed by tubular elongation of the receptacle, single style long-haired at base, twisted. Fr. a brown achene. March-July.

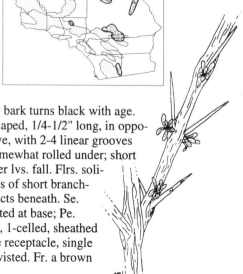

61

Mountain mahogany *(Cercocarpus)*

Rose Family (Rosaceae)

Key to species:

1 **A**—Leaves to 3/8" long; edges curled under to midrib . . . .
. . . . **Little-leaf mountain mahogany** *(C. intricatus)*
B—Leaves 3/8 to 1 1/2" long; edges rolled under, but not to midrib . . . . .
. . . . **Curl-leaf mountain mahogany** *(C. ledifolius)*

Distribution: Dry, rocky desert slopes. **Curl-leaf:** San Bern., Santa Rosa, San Jacinto Mtns. and mtns. of Mojave Desert, 4000-10,000'; PJW, SBS. **Little-leaf:** Mtns. of Mojave Desert; PJW.

Description: A 6-12' tall shrub or small tree, with a spreading crown, stout, branches. Older bark red-brown, furrowed. Lvs. alt., leathery, edges smooth and rolled under, blade hairless above, white-hairy below. Flrs. solitary or few-clustered, unstalked. Se. 5, united with receptacle into a tube, flaring at the mouth; Pe. none; St. many, in 2 or 3 rows; Ov. sup., 1-celled, the style elongated, feathery. Fr. an achene with a 2-3" long, twisted, feather-like tail. April- June.

MdW

Curl-leaf mtn. mahogany
(C. ledifolius) a.k.a.
Desert mtn. mahogany

fruit

Notes: The hard, heavy wood of Curl-leaf mtn. mahogany takes a high polish and is occasionally used for cabinet work.

Related species: **Mtn. mahogany** *(C. betuloides)*, a resident at lower elevations on the coastal side of our mountains, has oval, distinctly toothed leaves.

Elephant tree *(Bursera microphylla)*

a.k.a. Torote, Copal

Torchwood Family (Burseraceae)

Distribution: Restricted to s.w. corner of the Colorado Desert; CBS.

Description: A large aromatic shrub or small tree, 4-15' tall. Branches and trunk more or less swollen. Bark of young branches smooth and brown, that of older branches gray to cherry red, its thin, outer layer

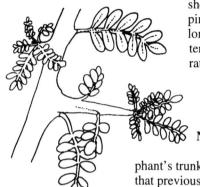

shedding. Lvs. alternate, 1-2" long, once-pinnately compound. Lflts. 11-35, about 1/4" long, falling during dry periods. Flrs. in clusters of 1-4. Se. 5, united below; Pe. 5, separate; St. 10, shorter than the petals; Ov. sup., 3-celled. Fr. a globular, 3-angled drupe that splits into 3 parts (valves) when mature. June, July.

Notes: Vernacular name derives from the swollen branches, suggesting an elephant's trunk. The bark contains aromatic chemicals that previously were collected in no. Mexico and burned as incense, called "copal," in churches. Frankincense and myrrh of biblical fame are derived from European members of the Torchwood Family. Indians thought the gum of the Elephant tree to have curative properties for sexually transmitted diseases.

Apricot mallow *(Sphaeralcea ambigua)*
a.k.a. Desert hollyhock, Desert mallow   Mallow Family (Malvaceae)

Distribution: Rocky canyons, slopes of both deserts below 4000'; CBS, JTW.

Description: A 1 1/2 - 4' high, bush with flexible, spreading stems, their bark covered with yellowish hairs; lower branches woody. Lvs. thickish, alt., palmately-veined, edges broadly 3-lobed; blade broad at base, narrowing to a blunt apex. Flrs. showy. Ca. 5-lobed, with 3 small bractlets below; Pe. 5, separate, 1/2 - 1 1/2" long, apricot-colored; St. many, the filaments fused into a tube around style; Ov. sup., many loculed, each with its own style. March - June.

Notes: This is sometimes called "sore-eye poppy," probably a translation of its Mexican name, *mal de ojos.* Its Pima Indian name means "a cure for sore eyes." Hopi Indians chew the stems much like chewing gum. Deer, pronghorns and bighorn sheep browse these plants.

Cupleaf ceanothus *(Ceanothus greggii)*

a.k.a. Gregg or Desert ceanothus   Buckthorn Family (Rhamnaceae)

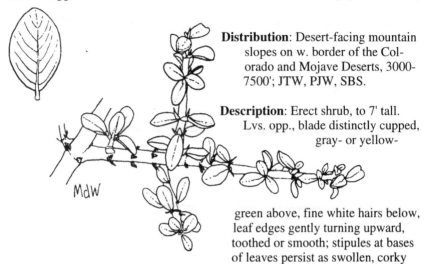

Distribution: Desert-facing mountain slopes on w. border of the Colorado and Mojave Deserts, 3000-7500'; JTW, PJW, SBS.

Description: Erect shrub, to 7' tall. Lvs. opp., blade distinctly cupped, gray- or yellow-green above, fine white hairs below, leaf edges gently turning upward, toothed or smooth; stipules at bases of leaves persist as swollen, corky bumps. Flrs. creamy white: Se. 5, petallike, joined at base with receptacle; Pe. 5, separate, tiny, narrowed at base, the sides of the broader tip folded together like a hood; St. 5, opp. petals; Ov. 3-celled, the style 3-parted. Fr. a 3-lobed capsule. May-June.

Notes: There are more kinds of *Ceanothus* in southern California than of any other native shrub, but only this one can be found on the desert-facing fringes, and there only on the mountain slopes, never on the desert floor.

Hoary coffeeberry *(Rhamnus tomentella)*

Buckthorn Family (Rhamnaceae)

Distribution: Shaded canyons in mountains of the Mojave Desert and on slopes of the Tehachapi, San Gabriel, San Bernardino, and Santa Rosa Mtns., mostly above 3500; Cha, CSS, JTW, PJW, CBS.

Description: Upright to spreading shrub, 6-12' tall, with reddish-brown twigs. Lvs. simple, alternate, evergreen, 1-3" long, half as wide, the edges smooth or minutely sawtoothed. Flrs. small, greenish, bisexual or unisexual, in clusters in the axils. Se. 4 or 5, united at base with receptacle; Pe. 5, tiny, shorter than sepals; St. 4 or 5, opposite petals; Ov. 2 to 4-celled. Fr. a red, then black, berrylike drupe. Apr. - June .

Notes: An extract of the bark was used by the Indians as a tonic. The bark was later harvested commercially and an extract sold as a laxative. Although the beans of coffeeberry look like those of the true coffee (hence its name), the resemblance to the popular beverage ends there; coffeeberry brew poses no threat to the coffee industry!

Hoary coffeeberry (con't)

Mdw

Coffeeberry shows a great deal of variation from one locality to the next, particularly in leaf shape and the presence or absence of hair on the blades. The form of this species growing in the mountains of the Mojave Desert is sufficiently different from the coastal form to be given a subspecific designation (*ursina*).

Lotebush *(Ziziphus parryi)*
a.k.a. Jujube, Parry condalia   Buckthorn Family (Rhamnaceae)

Distribution: Dry canyons, hillsides, 1200-3500', on Colorado Desert's western edge from Morongo Pass southward; JTW, PJW.

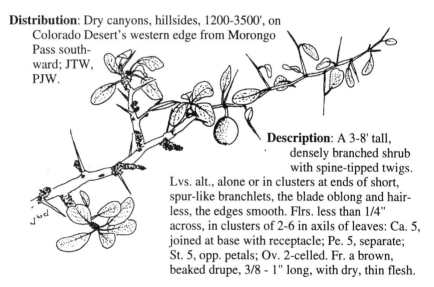

Description: A 3-8' tall, densely branched shrub with spine-tipped twigs. Lvs. alt., alone or in clusters at ends of short, spur-like branchlets, the blade oblong and hairless, the edges smooth. Flrs. less than 1/4" across, in clusters of 2-6 in axils of leaves: Ca. 5, joined at base with receptacle; Pe. 5, separate; St. 5, opp. petals; Ov. 2-celled. Fr. a brown, beaked drupe, 3/8 - 1" long, with dry, thin flesh.

Notes: The Cahuilla Indians pulverized the fruit and mixed the meal with water to make a gruel.

Related Species: Graythorn *(Z. obtusifolia)* is uncommon in the Sonoran Desert; its fruit is smaller (to 3/8"), beakless.

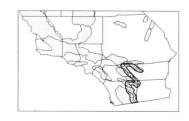

Bladderpod *(Isomeris arborea)*

a.k.a. Burro fat   Caper Family (Capparidaceae)

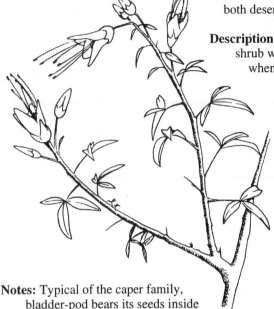

Distribution: Sandy washes throughout both deserts; CSS, CBS, JTW.

Description: A 2-9' tall, branching shrub with rank-smelling foliage when bruised. Lvs. alt., green-ish-yellow or grayish, 3-foliate (or simple below the flrs.), lflts. 1/2-1 1/2" long. Flrs. regular, in ter-minal racemes. Se. 4, fused at base; Pe. 4, sep-arate; St. 6, extending well beyond corolla; Ov. sup.,1-celled, on long, neck-like stalk. Fr. an inflated, 2-celled, 1-2" long capsule on 1-2" long stipe. Feb.- May but possible any time.

Notes: Typical of the caper family, bladder-pod bears its seeds inside an inflated capsule that resembles a fat pea pod. Another member of this family produces capers, the condiment used as a seasoning. Bladderpod has a taste reminiscent of radish but apparently was not eaten by the indigenous Indians. Its alternate name, burro fat, derives from its foul-smell, like that of a burro.

Bush peppergrass *(Lepidium fremontii)*

a.k.a. Desert alyssum   Mustard Family (Brassicaceae)

Distribution: Dry rocky soil of Mojave & no. Sonoran Desert, below 4500'; CBS, JTW.

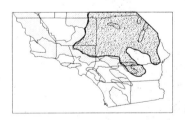

Description: A rounded shrub, 1-3' tall, with hairless branches. Lvs. alt., simple, almost without a petiole, 1 - 2 1/2" long, to 1/8" wide; upper lvs. linear, somewhat fleshy, the lower with 2 or 3 elongate lobes. Flrs. white, fragrant, on slender stalks in loose racemes: Se. 4; Pe. 4, separate, narrowed at base; St. 6, 2 shorter than the other 4; Ov. sup., 2-celled. Fr. a 2-celled capsule, roundish, notched above, about 1/4" across. March - May.

Notes: Many common vegetables belong to the Mustard Family: broccoli, cauliflower, cabbage, mustard, kohlrabi, radish, water cress and turnips, to

Bush peppergrass (con't)

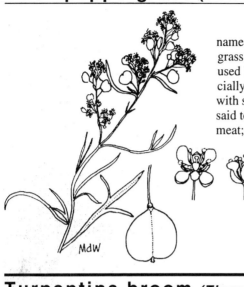

name a few. Seeds of Bush pepper-grass and several related species were used by Indians to flavor foods, especially salads, soups and stews. Mixed with salt and vinegar, the seeds are said to make a good marinade for meat; young leaves add "zip" to any salad. Peppergrass is one of the few members of the family that attains shrub status in southern California.

Turpentine broom *(Thamnosma montana)*
Rue Family (Rutaceae)

Distribution: Dry hills, below 5500'; CBS, JTW, PJW. .

Description: A strongly aromatic shrub, 1-2' tall, with yellowish-green, gland-dotted bark and spine-tipped stems. Lvs. alt., simple, 1/4-1/2" long, with smooth edges & no petiole; lvs. fall after a brief period leaving only naked, broom-like branches most of year. Flrs. 1/4-1/2" long, solitary along branches or in short racemes. Se. 4, fused at base; Pe. 4, dark purple, erect, spreading only slightly with age; St. 8, 4 long, 4 short; Ov. sup., 2-celled, its long style extending beyond the petals. Fr. a 2-lobed capsule, strong-smelling when crushed. Feb.- May.

fruit

Notes: The plants vernacular name derives from its strong odor and broom-like appearance. Some Arizona Indians used a decoction of the leaves as a "blood purifier" and as a treatment for gonorrhea.

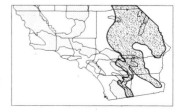

Sugar bush *(Rhus ovata)*

a.k.a. Sugar sumac   Sumac Family (Anacardiaceae)

Distribution: Mainly in the coastal foothills, below 4000', but reaching the w. edge of the Sonoran Desert; Cha, CSS, SOW, PJW .

Description: An erect evergreen shrub, 10 or 12' tall, with reddish twigs. Lvs. thickish, leathery with long petioles (3/8 - 1"); blades fold sharply upward at midrib to resemble taco shells; the edges smooth or irregularly sharp toothed, the tip pointed. Flrs. small, regular, white or pink, in panicles at ends of branches. Se. 5, joined at base; Pe. 5, distinct; St. 5; Ov. sup.,1-celled, with 3 styles. Fr. a red, sticky, softly hairy, semi-fleshy drupe. Mar. - May.

Squaw bush *(Rhus trilobata)*

Sumac Family (Anacardiaceae)

Distribution: Sporadic in desert canyons and washes'; Cha, CSS, SOW, RiW.

Description: A 3-5' tall, deciduous shrub, its branches often rooting where they contact the soil, its twigs usually brown. Lvs., compound, with 3 (rarely 5) leaflets, the terminal leaflet lacking a distinct petiole. Flrs. small, regular, in panicles at branch ends: Se. 5, joined at base; Pe. 5, distinct, yellowish; St. 5; Ov. sup., 1-celled, styles 3. Fr. a red, hairy, semi-fleshy, drupe. Mar. - May.

Notes: Indians used fruits to make a drink resembling pink lemonade. An approximation of the Indian beverage ("Rhus juice") can be made by adding ground, dried berries to water and sweetening it with honey. (But be careful; squaw bush is easily confused with Poison oak, a common plant of the coastal region!) Indians also used the plant's stems in the weaving of baskets and mats, hence its name.

68

Western sycamore *(Platanus racemosa)*

a.k.a. Plane tree, Buttonwood,
Buttonball tree

Sycamore Family (Platanaceae)

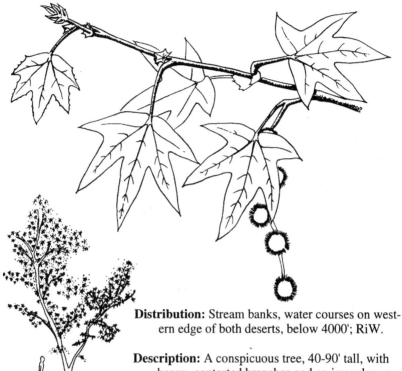

Distribution: Stream banks, water courses on western edge of both deserts, below 4000'; RiW.

Description: A conspicuous tree, 40-90' tall, with heavy, contorted branches and an irregular open crown. At base of trunk bark is thick, dark brown, furrowed; higher up it is thin, smooth, ashy-white, flaking to reveal green-gray, yellow, brown mottling. Lvs. alt., deciduous, palmately 3- to 5-lobed, edges of lobes smooth or with few large teeth; blade 5-10" long, 6-12" across, dense rusty haired when young, nearly hairless above when mature; petiole swollen at base, with conspicuous, sheathing stipules when young. Flrs. minute, clustered into dense, spherical, unisexual heads, male heads pea-sized, female heads 3-4 times as large. Male: Se. 3-6, scale-like; Pe. 3-6, papery; St. as many as petals. Female: Se. and Pe. 3-6 (usually 4); Ov. 1-celled, as many as sepals, with red styles and tufts of hair at base. Fr. a dense, globular head ("buttonball"), the nutlets buried among woolly hairs. Feb.- April.

Notes: On the coastal side of southern California's mountains Sycamore is one of the more common trees in streambed, but in deserts it is rare except along streams on their western edges. Though a good source of shade, the hairs of the leaves cause inflammation of the nasal chambers in sensitive persons.

Tamarisk *(Tamarix)*

a.k.a. Salt Cedar   Tamarisk Family (Tamaricaceae)

Distribution: Tamarisks are not California natives but many species grown for shade and as windbreaks have become naturalized in many parts of the desert. The plants are sufficiently common along roadways and stream beds that they seem a natural part of our desert flora. They are extremely hardy and can even endure the harsh conditions of alkali flats.

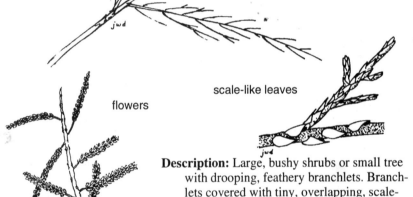

flowers

scale-like leaves

Description: Large, bushy shrubs or small tree with drooping, feathery branchlets. Branchlets covered with tiny, overlapping, scale-like leaves. Flrs. pink or white, in slender spikes at tips of branches. Se. 4-5; Pe. 4-5.

Notes: According to "The Jepson Manual: Higher Plants of California" the species growing in California include *T. aphylla, T chinensis, T. gallica, T. parviflora* and *T. ramosissima*. All look much alike, however, and are referred to by the same vernacular name. They were introduced from the Mediterranean region, probably in hay brought for horses by the Spaniards. A related species, *Tamarix mannifera*, in the middle east is reputed to be the source of "manna," the biblical "bread of heaven." Manna is, in reality, a sticky substance that exudes from insects, called plant lice, that suck the plant's juices. The droplets of sugary fluid falling on rocks crystallize into a substance not unlike honey in consistency and taste. Just as in biblical times, the Bedouins of the Sinai today gather manna, always early in the morning before ants emerge and take their bounty from them. Not only is manna a regular supplement to the Bedouin diet, the excess is exported.

Spiny senna *(Senna armata)*

Pea Family (Fabaceae)

Distribution: Sandy washes below 3700'; CBS.

Description: A rounded, many-branched shrub, 2-5' high, with yellow-green, mostly leaf-less stems with longitudinal lines. Lvs. pin-nately compound, 2 - 6" long, the rachis ending in a weak spine; lflts. 2 - 8, widely spaced, ovate or nearly round, 1/4" long. Flrs. regular, yel-low, showy, in 2 - 6" long racemes at branch ends: Se. 5, separate; Pe. 5, spreading, yellow to salmon; St. 10, 7 fertile, 3 sterile filaments.; Ov. sup., 1-celled. Fr. a many-seeded pod. April - July.

Notes: Though widely scattered through-out our deserts, Spiny senna is rarely noticed except when in bloom. Most of the year it is a mere cluster of leaf-less, greenish twigs.

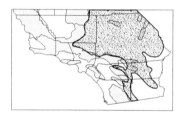

Rushpea *(Caesalpinia virgata)*

Pea Family (Fabaceae)

Distribution: Colorado Desert washes and canyons, below 4500'; CBS.

Description: A broad, rounded shrub, 2 - 4' (rarely 6') tall, with hairy, rush-like stems. Lvs. alt., scattered, gland-dotted, bipin-nately compound; pinnae 3, terminal pinna 1/2 - 1 1/4" long with 10 - 26 pinnules, lateral pinnae half as long with 8 - 18 pinnules. Flrs. about 3/8" long, almost reg-ular, in 4 - 6" long racemes: Ca. bell-shaped, 5-parted, hairy; Pe. 5, distinct, yellow, barely extending beyond calyx; St. 10, hairy, extend-ing beyond petals; Ov. sup., 1-celled. Fr. a flat, 1/2 - 1" long, curved, hairy pod. March - May.

Mesquite *(Prosopis)*

Pea Family (Fabaceae)

Key to species:

1 | **A**—Spines reach 1 1/4"; leaflets long, narrow, 7-17 pairs per pinna; pods flat or curved . . . . **Honey mesquite** *(P. glandulosa)*
   | **B**—Spines about 1/2" long; leaflets oblong, 5-11 pairs per pinna; pods tightly coiled like corkscrews . . . . . **Screwbean mesquite** *(P. pubescens)*

Distribution: Along streambeds, washes, and rivers, below 3000'; CBS.

Honey mesquite
(P. glandulosa)

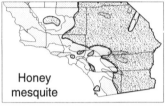

Honey mesquite

Description: Small trees or large shrubs to 20' (screwbean) or 30' (honey). Branches with paired spines. Lvs. with two pinnae, each with lflts. Flrs. small, regular, yellowish, in slender, cylindrical 2-3" long spikes. Se. 5, fused into bell-shaped calyx; Pe. 5, distinct; St. 10, extending well beyond corolla. Fr. a pod, ripening in fall. April - June.

Notes: Pods and foliage are browsed by livestock and large game; yet, mesquite spreads rapidly on overgrazed land. Wood is used for fence posts; hard, slow-burning, heartwood is ideal as firewood for BBQs. Bees attracted to flowers produce a distinctive honey.

Southwestern Indians relied heavily on pods of both species as a food staple, especially when cultivated crops failed. Pods were ground to make a meal (pinole) that was cooked into bread cakes or fermented to make an alcoholic beverage. Blossoms were roasted and eaten or brewed into a tea. The gummy sap of honey mesquite was eaten as a candy-like snack, used as a glue to mend pots, or packed on the head to remove lice and to dye the hair black. Fibers from inner bark were used in baskets and to make a coarse cloth.

Screwbean mesquite
(P. pubescens)
a.k.a. Tornillo

Screwbean mesquite

72

Palo verde *(Cercidium)*

Pea Family (Fabaceae)

Key to species:

1 | **A**—Leaves bipinnately compound, the main rachis obvious; pinnae 2, each with 1-3 pairs of leaflets; branches armed with short thorns; pod flat or slightly constricted between seeds . . . . **Blue palo verde** *(C. floridum)*
| **B**—Leaves bipinnately compound, the primary rachis very short or lacking; pinnae 2, each with 4-12 pairs of leaflets; branches without thorns but sharp-tipped; pod cylindric and decidedly constricted between seeds . . . .**Littleleaf palo verde** *(C. microphyllum)*

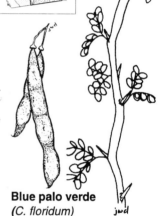

Distribution: Sandy washes; CBS. Blue p. v. is also planted along desert roadways. Littleleaf p. v. occurs only along the Colorado River near Whipple Mtns. (San Bern. Co.) and near the Mexican border.

Blue palo verde

Description: Large shrubs or small trees; to 25' (Littleleaf) or 35' (Blue). Bark green (palo verde is Spanish for "green stick"). Flrs. yellow, nearly regular, in axillary racemes. Se. 5, bell-shaped, turned backwards; Pe. 5, narrowed at base; St. 10, filaments hairy at base; Ov. sup., 1-celled. Fr. a pod. April - May (Littleleaf) or July (Blue).

Blue palo verde
(C. floridum)

Notes: Palo verdes are well-adapted to a water-limited existence. The leaves emerge after rains, then fall as the soil dries, leaving trees leafless most of year. Leaf drop diminishes water loss during the dry season but chlorophyll in bark permits photosynthesis to continue. Roots may go to 200 feet (8 times the height of tree) to reach water. Seeds germinate after being scarified (scratched) as they tumble along sandy washes during heavy rains. Indians ground seeds of both trees into flour eaten as a mush or baked into cakes. Flowers are visited by bees and yield a good honey. Wood is not a good firewood as it burns quickly with an unpleasant odor and leaves few coals.

Littleleaf palo verde
(C. microphyllum)
a.k.a. Yellow palo verde

Catclaw *(Acacia greggii)*

a.k.a. Devil's claw,
Wait-a-minute bush

Pea Family (Fabaceae)

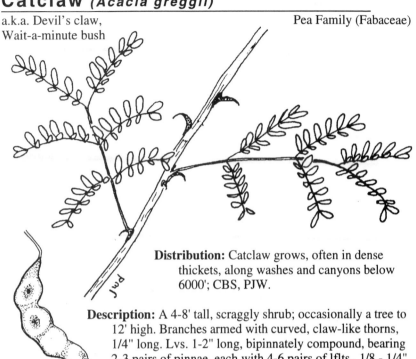

Distribution: Catclaw grows, often in dense thickets, along washes and canyons below 6000'; CBS, PJW.

Description: A 4-8' tall, scraggly shrub; occasionally a tree to 12' high. Branches armed with curved, claw-like thorns, 1/4" long. Lvs. 1-2" long, bipinnately compound, bearing 2-3 pairs of pinnae, each with 4-6 pairs of lflts., 1/8 - 1/4" long. Flrs. tiny, yellow, crowded on cylindrical spikes. Se. 5, usually fused; Pe. 5, separate; St. numerous, extending well beyond corolla; Ov. sup., 1-celled. Fr. a flattened pod, 2-6" long, somewhat constricted between the seeds. April - July.

Notes: The vernacular names of this shrub derive from its thorns. Not only do they resemble a cat's (or devil's?) claw but, when snagged on clothing and lacerating the flesh, often elicit the request that others "wait-a-minute."

Cattle consume the foliage in early spring. Many small birds and mammals find shelter among these natural armed fortresses. Indians consumed the pods after grinding them into flour. Pods and seeds are bitter; boiling pods or soaking beans overnight (discarding the water) makes them edible. Wood was used by Indians in construction of dwellings and for firewood.

Related species: Catclaw is our only native *Acacia*. Sweet acacia *(Acacia farnesiana)* has become naturalized near Otay, San Diego Co., probably introduced there by the Indians. Sweet acacia is easily separated from catclaw by its location, its long, straight spines, and it 10-25 pair of leaflets per pinna.

Smoke tree *(Psorothamnus spinosus)*
a.k.a. Smokethorn, Tree pea   Pea Family (Fabaceae)

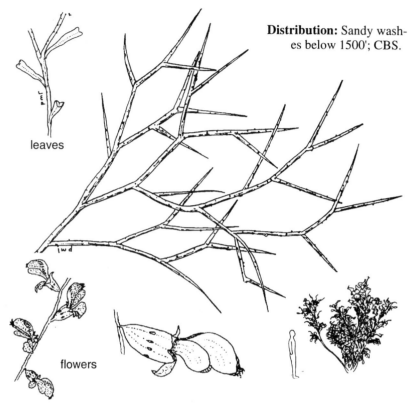

Distribution: Sandy washes below 1500'; CBS.

leaves

flowers

Description: An intricately branched small tree or shrub, 6-30' high. Branches nearly leafless, spine-tipped, ash-gray, dotted with brownish glands. Lvs. few, simple, almost petioleless, 1/4 - 1" long, remaining on tree only short time. Flrs. pea-like, fragrant, in terminal spikes. Ca. 5-toothed, densely hairy, with reddish glands; Pe. 5, dark blue, narrowed at base, the banner heart-shaped; St. 10, filaments united into a tube; Ov. sup., 1-celled;. Fr. a gland-dotted pod. May - July.

Notes: When viewed from a distance, especially at dawn or dusk, this tree often resembles a puff of smoke, hence its common name. In early summer, a profusion of flowers provides a striking contrast to the plant's usual monotonous gray. The plant's high water requirements restrict it

to desert washes. Its seeds germinate only after being scratched by tumbling in the sand during spring rains, assuring an abundant, albeit temporary, supply of water for its germinating seedlings.

Indigo bush *(Psorothamnus)*

Pea Family (Fabaceae)

Key to species:

1   A—Flowers blue-purple, in loose clusters 2" long or longer; pods extend
      beyond mouth of calyx . . . . Go to 2
     B—Flowers pale rose to lavender, in tight clusters, mostly less than 1/2"
      long; pods do not extend beyond mouth of calyx . . . . Go to 4

2   A—Leaves simple, linear; Colorado Des. . **Schott indigo bush** *(P. schottii)*
     B—Leaves compound; plant of the Mojave Desert or northern (higher) por-
      tion of Colorado Desert. . . . . Go to 3

3   A—Fruit hairless, with many small glands arranged in lines; plant of eastern
      half of Mojave Desert . . . . **Fremont indigo bush** *(P. fremontii)*
     B—Fruit hairless or finely hairy, with large, scattered glands; plant of west-
      ern half of the Mojave Desert . . **Mojave indigo bush** *(P. arborescens)*

4   A—Plant green; leaves, stems only moderately hairy; terminal leaflet round-
      tipped; Mojave Des., above 2500' . **Nevada indigo bush** *(P. polydenius)*
     B—Plant whitish; leaves, stems with dense white hairs; terminal leaflet
      pointed; Colorado Des., below 1000' . . **Emory indigo bush** *(P. emoryi)*

Schott indigo bush
(P. schottii) a.k.a.
Schott or Mesa
Dalea

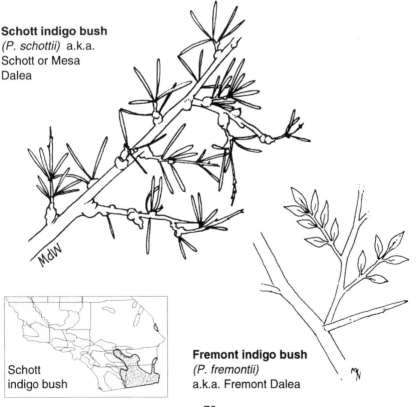

Schott
indigo bush

Fremont indigo bush
(P. fremontii)
a.k.a. Fremont Dalea

76

Indigo bush (con't)

Nevada indigo bush

Emory indigo bush

Distribution: Washes, adjacent flatlands; CBS (all), SbS, JTW (Fremont, Nev.).

Description: Intricately branched, 4-6' (10' in Schott) tall. Flrs. in loose racemes or spikes; flrs. much like those of Smoke Tree (preceding page).

Notes: All indigo bushes were sources of dyes for desert-dwelling Indians. A tea made from the boiled stems of a Nevada indigo bush was used to treat coughs and influenza. Stems were reportedly chewed for toothache.

Ironwood *(Olneya tesota)*

Pea Family (Fabaceae)

Distribution: Washes of the Colorado Desert, below 2000'; CBS.

Description: A tree with spreading crown, 15-35' tall. Bark thin, scaly. A pair of spines below once-pinnately compound lvs; lflts. 8-24, covered with soft, grayish hairs. Flrs. pea-like, in short racemes. Ca. 5-lobed, bell-shaped; Pe. 5, purple, attached by short, narrow neck, banner roundish; St.10, their filaments united into 2 sets; Ov. many-chambered. Fr. a hairy, glandular pod.

Notes: Ironwood grows only in the warmer desert regions, hence is considered a good indicator of a climate suitable for citrus. The wood is extremely dense and hard, so much so that it does not float. Indians used the wood to make arrowheads. They also ate the peanut-flavored seeds after parching them or grinding them to flour from which they made a gruel or cake. Bighorn sheep and mule deer browse the plant.

Mexican palo verde *(Parkinsonia aculeata)*

a.k.a. Horse-bean,
Jerusalem-thorn

Pea Family (Fabaceae)

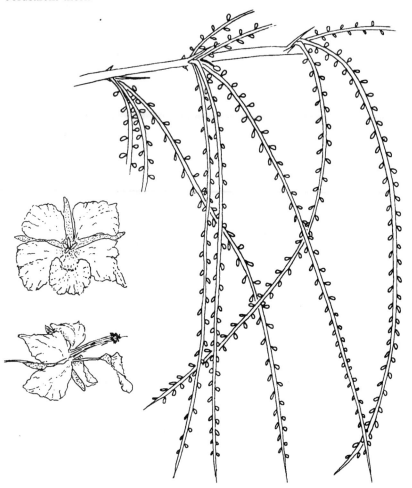

Distribution: This plant is not native to California, but is commonly planted
along desert roadways. In some areas it has become naturalized.

Description: Large shrubs or small trees to 40' tall with yellow-green, smooth
bark. Branches armed with triplets of reddish spines at each node. Lvs.
bipinnately compound, but the common rachis is often almost non-exis-
tent; hence pinnae appear to be paired, once-pinnate, lvs. Rachis of pinnae
broad, flat, up to 24" long; lflts. tiny, numerous but falling early leaving
rachis as a long streamer. Flrs. somewhat irregular, showy, in elongate
racemes. Se. 5, turning backward; Pe. 5, yellow, one (banner) turning red
with age; St. 10. Fr. a bulging pod constricted between seeds.

78

Adonis lupine *(Lupinus excubitus)*

Pea Family (Fabaceae)

Distribution: Rocky places, mostly above 4000' in mtns. along desert borders; CBS, PJW, Cha, CSS, YPF.

Description: An erect or rounded, leafy shrub, 2 - 5' tall. Lvs. alt., palmately compound, petioles 2-4" long; lflts. 7 - 9, 3/4 - 2" long, with dense, fine silky hairs on both surfaces, the edges smooth. Flrs. papilionaceous, blue, violet or orchid, in racemes at ends of branches: Ca. 2-lipped; Co. of 5 petals, a sail-like banner, hairless or with short downy hairs on its back, two hairless wings, a keel of 2 fused petals with minute hairs along edges; St. 10, the filaments united into a tube; Ov. sup., 1-celled. Fr. a flat pod. March - July.

Notes: Lupines get their name from *Lupus,* Latin for wolf, because they were thought to rob the soil of its fertility; in fact, they do quite the opposite, adding essential nutrients to the soil. Taxonomically the lupines are particularly difficult, creating problems for experts and amateurs alike. This species is so variable that experts subdivide it into five subspecies that vary greatly in leaf color and hairiness, and ranging from the desert to the coast and high into the mountains. This is the only bush lupine normally associated with deserts.

Broom lotus *(Lotus rigidus)*

Pea Family (Fabaceae)

Distribution: Dry washes and slopes, below 5000', in both deserts; CBS, PJW JTW.

Description: A low shrub, 1 - 2 1/2" high, with rigid, erect stems. Lvs. alt., pinnately compound, 3/8 - 3/4" long, widely spaced; lflts. 3 - 5, narrowly oblong. Flrs. pea-like, 1/2 - 3/4" long, in clusters of 2 - 3 at ends of 2 - 5" long stalks: Ca. 5-toothed; Pe. 5, yellow, turning red to purple with age; St. 10, 9 united by filaments, 1 free; Ov. sup., 1-celled. Fr. a 3/4 - 2" long pod. March - May.

Related species: Many kinds of lotus occur in southern California, but most scarcely qualify as shrubs. Deerweed *(L. scoparius)* is a common shrub of the chaparral.

Fairy duster *(Calliandra eriophylla)*

a.k.a. False Mesquite   Pea Family (Fabaceae)

Distribution: Sandy stream-
beds, below 1000'; CBS.

Description: Densely branched, 1/2-3'
tall, shrub. Lvs. alt., bipinnately
compound, 1-4 pr. pinnae, these
with 5-12 pr. pinnules, ea. 1/8" long
or less. Flrs. showy, in dense few-
flowered heads: Ca. 5-toothed, red-
brown; Pe. 5, dark red, united to
middle into funnel-shaped corolla;
St. many, red, up to 1" long, joined
at base, extending well beyond corolla; Ov. sup., 1-celled. Fr. a 2 - 2 1/2"
long, red-margined pod covered with silvery hairs. Feb. - May.

Sandpaper plant *(Petalonyx thurberi)*

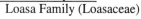

Loasa Family (Loasaceae)

Distribution: Sandy washes and fans
of both deserts below 4000'; CBS.

Description: A 1-3' tall, spreading,
woody-based bush. Lvs. triangular-
shaped, 1/4-1" long, the blade
attached to stem by its broad base; edge
smooth or sometimes toothed at base.
Leaf surface with numerous stiff, barbed
hairs, sandpapery. Flrs. white or yellowish, in dense spikes at ends of branches;
greenish bracts, toothed at base,
below spikes. Se. 5, fused at base
to ovary; Pe. 5, their long, narrow
bases appearing united into a tube,
the broad tips flaring; St. 5, extending beyond petals; Ov. inf.,1-
celled. May - July.

Related species: Two other species of
sandpaper plant also occur on our
deserts, but are much less common.

flowering stalk

flower

Sandpaper plant (con't)

Smooth sandpaper plant, *P. nitidus*, is found in the mountains of the Mojave Desert, between 3500-6500'; its finely sandpapery leaves have a distinct petiole. Narrowleaf sandpaper plant, *P. linearis*, occurs below 3000' in rocky canyons of the Colorado Desert and the southeastern Mojave Desert. The edges of its rough-feeling leaves are always smooth, the blades attached by a narrowed base.

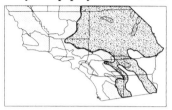

Rhatany *(Krameria)*

Krameria Family (Krameriaceae)

Key to species:

1 | **A**—Sepals pink, cupped upward; 3 upright petals fused at base; spines on fruit lack barbs or have barbs all along shaft . **Pima rhatany** *(K. erecta)*
   | **B**—Sepals deep purple-red, folded backwards; 3 upright petals separate; fruit spines with barbs only at tip . . . . **White rhatany** *(K. grayi)*

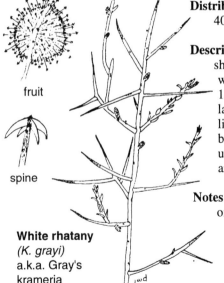

fruit

spine

White rhatany
(K. grayi)
a.k.a. Gray's
krameria

Distribution: Dry, rocky areas, below 4000'; CBS.

Description: Intricately branched, thorny shrub, 1 -2' tall, young branches soft, white woolly. Lvs. alt., simple, 1/8 - 1/2" long, linear (Pima) or narrowly lance-shaped (White). Se. 5, petal-like; Pe. 5, 3 above erect, elongate, 2 below smaller, glandular; St. 4, in unequal pairs; Ov. sup., 1-celled. Fr. armed with long spines. April - Sept.

Notes: Both rhatanies are partial parasites on the roots of other shrubs, including Burro-weed *(Ambrosia dumosa)* and Creosote *(Larrea tridentata)*. Livestock and deer browse these plants and disseminate the seeds.

White rhatany

Pima rhatany

Ocotillo *(Fouquieria splendens)*

a.k.a. Coachwhip,
Slimwood, Candlewood

Ocotillo Family (Fouquieriaceae)

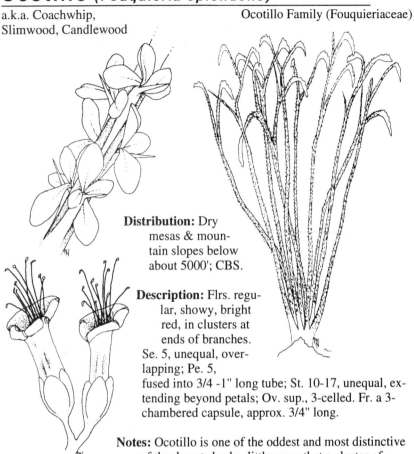

Distribution: Dry mesas & mountain slopes below about 5000'; CBS.

Description: Flrs. regular, showy, bright red, in clusters at ends of branches. Se. 5, unequal, overlapping; Pe. 5, fused into 3/4 -1" long tube; St. 10-17, unequal, extending beyond petals; Ov. sup., 3-celled. Fr. a 3-chambered capsule, approx. 3/4" long.

Notes: Ocotillo is one of the oddest and most distinctive of the desert shrubs, little more that a cluster of cane-like, mostly unbranched stems rising 15-20' from the ground. Branches are armed with stiff, straight thorns, remnants of the petioles of the primary leaves. Secondary leaves appear at the bases of the thorns after rains, falling when the soil dries, thus restricting water loss. Chlorophyll in the bark allows plant to photosynthesize while leafless. Scarlet blossoms at the tips of the branches lend a festive air to the desert when the plant flowers in late spring.

Ocotillo is commonly grown as an ornamental or in rows as a living fence. Desert-dwelling Indians used stems in constructing dwellings; a decoction of the root was used to treat swellings and fatigue. Capsules and flowers are edible; a beverage can be made by soaking the flowers overnight. Wax from the stems has been used to dress leather.

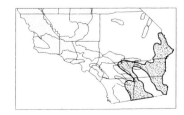

Yerba santa *(Eriodictyon)*

Waterleaf Family (Hydrophyllaceae)

Key to species:

1   A—Young stems and upper leaf surface with a silky mat of downy hair . . .
     . . . . **Thickleaf yerba santa** *(E. crassifolium)*
     B—Young stems and upper leaf surface smooth, mostly hairless, sticky . . .
     . . . . **Smoothleaf yerba santa** *(E. trichocalyx)*

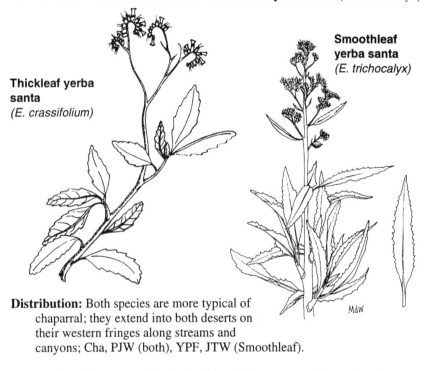

Thickleaf yerba santa
(E. crassifolium)

Smoothleaf yerba santa
(E. trichocalyx)

MdW

Distribution: Both species are more typical of chaparral; they extend into both deserts on their western fringes along streams and canyons; Cha, PJW (both), YPF, JTW (Smoothleaf).

Description: Erect, aromatic shrubs, 2-8' tall, leaves crowded at ends of branches. Lvs. alt.,thick, leathery, lance-shaped, 2-6" long, edges coarsely toothed. Flrs. lavender to white, borne on one side of a coiled cluster (cyme) at ends of branches: Ca. deeply 5-lobed; Co. 5-parted, funnel-shaped, 1/4 - 3/4" long (Thickleaf) or half as long (Smoothleaf); St. 5; Ov. sup., 2-celled, styles 2. Fr. a 4-valved capsule. April - June.

Notes: The vernacular name of these plants, meaning "holy herb," was given by the Spanish padres because of their supposed medicinal properties. Indeed, a bitter tea made from the dried leaves of either species is said to be a good expectorant and to relieve sore throat and cough. Indians used mashed leaves on sores, cuts and infections.

Related species: Narrowleaf yerba santa, *E. angustifolium,* is uncommon in the New York Mtns. in the eastern Mojave Desert. The edges of its nearly hairless, sticky leaves are smooth or nearly so.

Desert thorn *(Lycium)*

Nightshade Family (Solanaceae)

Key to species: (Even specialists have difficulty with this group. Only when in flower or fruit is positive identification possible.)

1 | **A**—Calyx lobes at least 2/3 as long as calyx tube, 1/16" or longer . . Go to 2
  | **B**—Calyx lobes half or less the length of the calyx tube . . . . . . .Go to 4

2 | **A**—Flowers are less than 3/8" long, pink to violet, often with black stripes in throat; berry is soft and red . . . . **Desert thorn** *(L. brevipes)*
  | **B**—Flowers are mostly longer than 3/8", white, greenish or lavender; berry is hard, not red . . . . Go to 3

3 | **A**—Flowers are white or lavender, to 3/4" long; berry is green-purple to white . . . . **Rabbit thorn** *(L. pallidum)*
  | **B**—Flowers greenish-white with lavender veins, to 1/2" long; berry green and grooved around middle . . . . **Boxthorn** *(L. cooperi)*

4 | **A**—Petal lobes woolly, fringed with tiny white hairs; some leaf blades as long as 2"; as wide as 3/8" . . . . **Squaw thorn** *(L. torreyi)*
  | **B**—Petal lobes either hairless or with only tiny hairs; leaf blades not much exceeding 1" in length, 1/4" in width . . . . .Go to 5

5 | **A**—Leaf blades densely hairy; some leaf blades as long a 1", as wide as 1/4" . . . . **Fremont desert thorn** *(L. fremontii)*
  | **B**—Leaf blade hairless, fleshy; most leaf blades shorter than 5/8", always less than 1/8" wide . . . . **Anderson desert thorn** *(L. andersonii)*

Distribution: Boxthorn and Anderson desert thorn occur in rocky places, below 5000' and 6000', respectively; CBS, JTW, PJW (both), SBS, Cha, CSS (Anderson only). Desert thorn and Fremont desert thorn occupy washes, alkaline places and hillsides of the Colorado Desert, below 1500'; CBS, AlS. Squaw thorn occurs in Colorado and sw. Mojave Desert, below 2000', Rabbit thorn in central and no. Mojave Desert, below 2500'; CBS.

Description: Erect shrubs armed with stout spines. Lvs. alt., simple, smooth-edged, small ones often clustered in axils of larg-er. Flrs. regular, solitary or in clusters of 2 to 6 on short pedicels. Se. 5, united into a tubular or bell-shaped calyx; Pe. 5 (rarely 4 or 6), fused into a tubular or funnel-

Fremont desert thorn

shaped corolla, the lobes spreading; St. attached to petals, one per petal, often hairy at base; Ov. sup., 2-celled, with bilobed stigma. Fr. a 2- to many-seeded berry. March - May or June.

Related Species: Parish desert thorn *(L. parishii)* is rare in California, found only in a few isolated canyons in the Colorado Desert.

Desert thorn (con't)

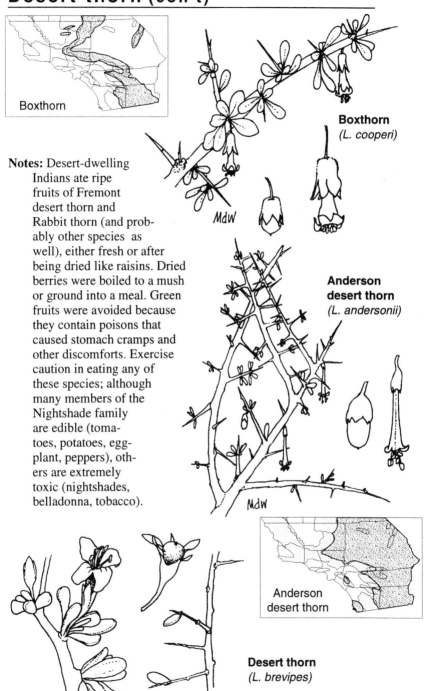

Boxthorn

Boxthorn
(L. cooperi)

MdW

Notes: Desert-dwelling Indians ate ripe fruits of Fremont desert thorn and Rabbit thorn (and probably other species as well), either fresh or after being dried like raisins. Dried berries were boiled to a mush or ground into a meal. Green fruits were avoided because they contain poisons that caused stomach cramps and other discomforts. Exercise caution in eating any of these species; although many members of the Nightshade family are edible (tomatoes, potatoes, eggplant, peppers), others are extremely toxic (nightshades, belladonna, tobacco).

Anderson desert thorn
(L. andersonii)

MdW

Anderson desert thorn

Desert thorn
(L. brevipes)

Wild grape *(Vitis girdiana)*

Grape Family (Vitaceae)

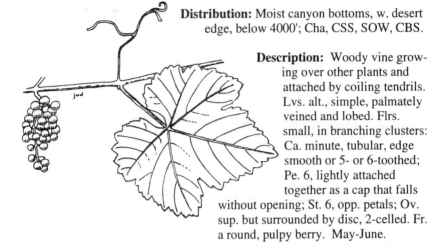

Distribution: Moist canyon bottoms, w. desert edge, below 4000'; Cha, CSS, SOW, CBS.

Description: Woody vine growing over other plants and attached by coiling tendrils. Lvs. alt., simple, palmately veined and lobed. Flrs. small, in branching clusters: Ca. minute, tubular, edge smooth or 5- or 6-toothed; Pe. 6, lightly attached together as a cap that falls without opening; St. 6, opp. petals; Ov. sup. but surrounded by disc, 2-celled. Fr. a round, pulpy berry. May-June.

Notes: Readily recognized, this plant closely resembles its cultivated cousin. The purple fruits can be eaten fresh or dried as raisins. The edible leaves can be used to wrap other foods. Raw tendrils make a pleasant snack. Indians made wine from the grapes and used juice of leaves to treat "lust" in women.

Bedstraw *(Galium angustifolium)*

a.k.a. Cleavers, Goosegrass   Madder Family (Rubiaceae)

Distribution: Shaded places below 8000'; Cha, CSS, SOW, YPF, CBS, JTW.

Description: A semi-shrubby, 1-4' tall, often sprawling plant; base and lower branches woody. Stems slender, 4-angled, hairless to densely armed with curved bristly hairs. Lvs. simple, in whorls of 4 (2 are really stipules), strap-shaped, to 1" long, the whorls 1 - 3" apart along stem. Flrs. small, cream to greenish, regular, abundant; Se. 4, scarcely evident; Co. 4-parted; St. 4, short; Ov. inf., 2-lobed. Fr. two dry, bristly-haired halves.

Notes: Pioneers used dried stems as mattress stuffing. A tea from plant is said to relieve urinary tract disorders. Dried, roasted seeds can be used as a coffee substitute; the taste is even said to resemble that of coffee, not surprisingly since coffee belongs to the same family. A useful purple dye can be extracted from the roots.

Desert-willow *(Chilopsis linearis)*

a.k.a. Desert catalpa   Bignonia Family (Bignoniaceae)

Distribution: Stream-beds of Colorado and so. Mojave Deserts; CBS, JTW.

Description: A sprawling shrub or small tree, 6-20' tall. Branches slender, willowlike. Lvs. alternate (lower ones often opposite), simple, very long (4-6") and narrow (usually less than 1/4"), often curved like a sickle, lacking a distinct petiole. Flrs. large and showy, more-or-less 2-lipped, clustered at ends of branches. Se. 5, fused and inflated, upper lip with 3 teeth, the lower with 2; Pe. 5, fused into 1-2" long, funnel, pink or white,

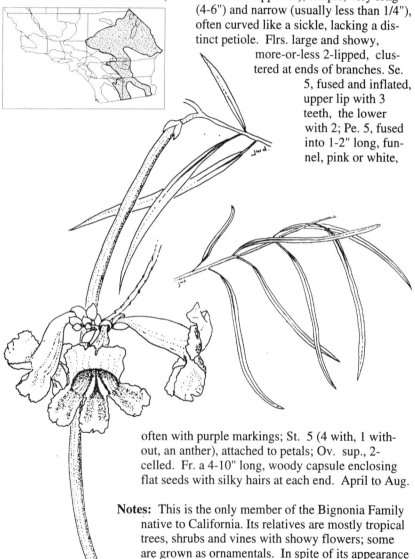

often with purple markings; St. 5 (4 with, 1 without, an anther), attached to petals; Ov. sup., 2-celled. Fr. a 4-10" long, woody capsule enclosing flat seeds with silky hairs at each end. April to Aug.

Notes: This is the only member of the Bignonia Family native to California. Its relatives are mostly tropical trees, shrubs and vines with showy flowers; some are grown as ornamentals. In spite of its appearance and vernacular name, this is not a true willow. A sort of tea is sometimes brewed from the dried flowers and seed pods.

Desert sages *(Salvia)*

Mint Family (Lamiaceae)

Key to species:

1   A—Flowers few, in pairs of loose, branching clusters opposite each other, the corolla white, spotted with lavender; lower leaves up to 4" long; plant growing on mountain slopes fringing the deserts on the west . . . . **White sage** *(S. apiana)*

     B—Flowers many, in compact whorls forming an interrupted spike, the corolla not as above; leaves rarely exceeding 2 1/2" in length . . Go to 2

2   A—Plants growing in Colorado Desert . . . . Go to 3

     B—Plants growing in the Mojave Desert or above 5000' in the mountains fringing the deserts . . . . Go to 5

3   A—Flowers white, in whorls subtended by white, bristle-tipped bracts; leaves up to 2 1/2" long, mostly crowded near the base of wand-like branches; plant grows on the western edge of the Colorado Desert below 2500' . . . . **Brittle sage** *(S. vaseyi)*

     B—Flowers blue, lavender or rose and bracts beneath the whorls, if present, not as above; leaves mostly shorter than 1 1/4" . . . . Go to 4

4   A—Leaves broadly egg-shaped, with 3-6 long, spine-tipped teeth on the edges, the upper surface of blade green with densely matted hairs; flowers pale lavender in mostly incomplete whorls without colored bracts; plant occurs in the vicinity of the Salton Sea below 600' . . . . **Orocopia sage** *(S. greatae)*

     B—Leaves more or less lance-shaped, edged with minute, rounded teeth, the upper surface markedly blistered or puckered; flowers pale blue to rose, in complete whorls, each whorl underlain by thin, roundish, purplish-green bracts; plant grows along the western edge of the Colorado Desert, 1200-4500' . . . . **Desert sage** *(S. eremostachya)*.

5   A—Whorls of dark, violet-blue flowers underlain by showy, purple to rose bracts up to 3/4" long with hair-fringed edges; leaf blade often exceeding 1" in length, minutely hairy on both surfaces; plant grows from 5000 to 10,000' in the mtns. of the eastern Mojave Desert or on the desert-facing slopes of the Tehachapis, the San Bernardino Mtns., and southward . . . . **Mountain desert sage** *(S. pachyphylla)*

     B—Bracts and flowers not as above; leaf blade rarely exceeding 3/4" in length, the upper surface either hairless or finely wrinkled . . . Go to 6

6   A—Upper leaf surface smooth; flowers blue, in 3-4 whorls on each flower stem, each whorl underlain with purplish or greenish, membranous, rounded bracts; plant grows from 2500 to 8800' in the mountains fringing the Mojave Desert . . . . **Purple desert sage** *(S. dorrii)*

     B—Upper surface of leaves finely wrinkled; flowers lavender in mostly solitary whorls, each underlain by white, membranous bracts; plant occurs from 1000 to 5000' in Mojave Desert . . . **Mojave sage** *(S. mojavensis)*

Desert sages (con't)

Distribution: Mostly on dry, gravelly, slopes of desert canyons, washes and fans. White sage, more typical of the coastal region, barely enters the deserts at their fringes; Cha, CSS, SOW, PJW, YPF. Colorado Desert species; CBS. Mojave sage; CBS, JTW. Purple desert sage: CBS, JTW, SBS, YPF. Mountain desert sage; PJW, YPF.

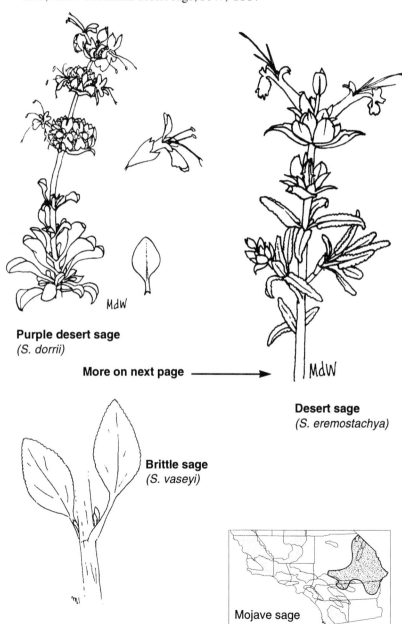

Purple desert sage
(S. dorrii)

More on next page ⟶

Desert sage
(S. eremostachya)

Brittle sage
(S. vaseyi)

Mojave sage

MdW

Mountain desert sage
(S. pachyphylla)

White sage
(S. apiana)

Description: Sages are aromatic, compact, much-branched shrubs, mostly 2' or shorter but White sage reaches 6'. Stems squarish. Lvs. opp., simple. Flrs. irregular. Ca. tubular, 2-lipped; Co. tubular, strongly 2-lipped, the lower lip 3-lobed, spreading; St. 4, lower pair fertile, upper pair sterile or rudimentary; Ov. sup., 4-lobed. Fr. 4 smooth nutlets. March - June (most species), May - July (Desert sage), April -Sept. (White sage).

Related species: Black sage *(S. mellifera)*, though more typical of the coastal foothills, occasionally occurs on the fringes of our deserts.

Notes: Bees feed heavily on the flowers of all the sages. The leaves of many species were used by early settlers to brew a tea and as a seasoning in many meat dishes. Indians gathers the seeds of white sage and ground them into a flour. Despite the strong, almost rank, odor of white sage many animals browse on it, especially during summer.

Mountain blue curls *(Trichostema parishii)*

Mint Family (Lamiaceae)

Distribution: Dry desert slopes of transverse
range, 2000 to 6000'; JTW, Cha, YPF.

Description: Strongly aromatic shrub, to
about 4' tall. Lvs. simple, opp., long
(to about 2") and narrow, lacking
petioles, the lower surface densely
woolly, smaller leaves usually clustered in axils
of larger. Flrs. in spikes (6" or more long) of
axillary cymes, each cyme of one to many
flowers; flrs. borne on short stems at
right angles from main stem. Flowering
stem and calyces woolly. Ca. equally 5-
cleft; Co. a 2-lipped tube, both lips 2-
lobed, the tube to 3/8" long; St. 4, arched,
less than 1" long; Ov. sup., 4-celled. Fr. 4
rough surfaced nutlets. May - August.

Notes: Early California settlers made a liniment
from the leaves that was used in the treatment of bruises and sore muscles.

Desert-lavender *(Hyptis emoryi)*

a.k.a. Bee sage,
Emory bushmint

Mint Family (Lamiaceae)

Distribution: Ravines and rocky hillsides below 3000' in
Colorado and s. Mojave Deserts; CBS.

Description: Erect, 3-10' tall, sweet-smelling shrub. Lvs.
opp., simple, 1/4 - 1" long, blade broader at base
than at tip, thickly covered with whitish hairs; edges
with fine, rounded teeth. Flrs. irregular, densely clustered in axils of small lvs. near ends of
branchlets. Ca. with 5 bristle-tipped teeth,
densely covered with woolly hair; Co.
pale purple, 2-lipped, the middle lower
lip expanded like a bag; St. 4, the anthers
encased by bag-like portion of the lower
lip, filaments of upper two hairy; Ov.
sup., 4-celled. Fr. 4 nutlets. March -
May.

MdW

Notes: Bees commonly visit the fragrant flowers, making the alternate name
"bee sage" quite apt. In Mexico, seeds of this plant are eaten under the
name "chia."

Bladder sage *(Salazaria mexicana)*

a.k.a. Paper-bag bush   Mint Family (Lamiaceae)

Distribution: Washes, hillsides, rocky canyons below 5000'; CBS, JTW.

Description: A straggly, 1 1/2 - 4' tall shrub. Lvs. opp., simple, 1/4 - 3/4" long, the edges smooth or sometimes irregularly toothed; crushed lvs. strongly aromatic. Flrs. irregular, 2-4" long, in few-flowered, spike-like clusters. Ca. tubular, 2-lipped, inflated when in fruit; Co. 2-lipped, cream-colored except for purple lower lip; St. 4; Ov. sup., 4-lobed. Fr. 4 nutlets enclosed in bladder-like calyx. March-June.

Notes: This shrub when in fruit is easily distinguished from all others in southern California by its papery, bag-like calyxes resembling Chinese lanterns. Many rodents extract and eat the seeds.

Chuparosa *(Justicia californica)*

Acanthus Family (Acanthaceae)

Distribution: Sandy watercourses on w. and n. perimeters of the Colorado Desert; CBS.

Description: An almost leafless, 2-5' high shrub with straggly, gray-green branches. Lvs. 1/4-1" long, opp., simple, ovate, falling in dry season; leaf edge smooth. Flrs. dull red, densely clustered, a single, small bract at the base of each. Se. 5, united at base; Pe. 5, fused into a 2-lipped tube, 1 -1 1/4" long; St. 2, anthers extending beyond corolla's upper lip; Ov. sup., 2-celled. Fr. club-shaped capsule. Feb. - June (often later).

Notes: Desert hummingbirds suck nectar from the flowers of this plant. Common name comes from "chupar," Spanish meaning to suck. The cucumber-flavored flowers are eaten by the Papago Indians and sucked for their nectar by others.

Burro-weed & Bursage *(Ambrosia)*

Sunflower Family (Asteraceae)

Key to species:

1 **A**—Leaves to 3/4" long, 1-3 times pinnately divided into short, rounded lobes, whitish with soft, downy hairs; female heads usually 2-flowered; male heads about 1/8" across; fruit a spiny bur, to 3/16" long; abundant throughout both deserts . . . . **Burro-weed** *(A. dumosa)*

   B—Leaves to 1" long, the blade lance-shaped with several short rounded lobes, green above with patches of short hairs, whitish, densely hairy below; female heads usually one-flowered; male heads 1/4 - 1/2" across, densely hairy; fruit a white, woolly bur, to 3/8" long, with up to 20 straight spines; locally common in New York and Providence Mtns. . . . . **Woolly bursage** *(A. eriocentra)*

Distribution: Sandy mesas, plains to 4000' (Burro-weed), dry washes, slopes, 2500-4000' (Woolly bursage); CBS, JTW (both) PJW (Bursage).

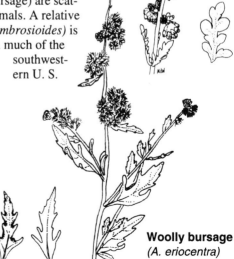

Burro-weed
(A. dumosa)
a.k.a White bursage,
Sandbur

Description: Shrubs, low, rounded, to 2' (Burro-weed); spreading, to 3' tall, its twigs with few long, many short hairs (Woolly bursage). March - May (Burro-weed occasionally at other times after rains).

Notes: Burro-weed is a common associate of creosote bush throughout our deserts. It is browsed by many wild animals and by burros and cattle. Its burred seeds (and those of woolly bursage) are scattered by clinging to fur of animals. A relative of these plants, ragweed *(A. ambrosioides)* is a significant hayfever plant in much of the southwestern U. S.

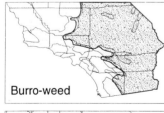

Burro-weed

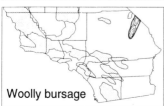

Woolly bursage

Woolly bursage
(A. eriocentra)

93

Brittlebush, Encelia *(Encelia)*

Sunflower Family (Asteraceae)

Key to species:

1 **A**—Leaves to 3" long, densely soft white-hairy, appearing gray-green to silvery; flowering stalks often branched; common throughout both deserts
. . . . **Brittlebush** *(E. farinosa)*
B—Leaves scarcely reaching 1 1/2", leaves finely hairy or sparsely stiff-haired, green; flowering stalks unbranched . . . . Go to 2

2 **A**—Leaves entirely stiff haired, rough to the touch; heads lacking ray flower; occasional in both deserts. . . . . **Bush encelia** *(E. frutescens)*
B—Leaves mostly fine-haired, occasionally with stouter hairs interspersed; heads with ray flowers . . . . Go to 3

3 **A**—Leaves soft, silvery haired throughout; ray flowers up to 1" long; plant of western desert edge and mountains of southern Mojave Desert . . . .
. . . . **Acton encelia** *(E. actoni)*
B—Leaves with stiff hairs intermixed with softer hairs; ray flowers mostly less than 5/8" long; plant of the eastern Mojave Desert . . . .
. . . . **Virginia City encelia** *(E. virginensis)*

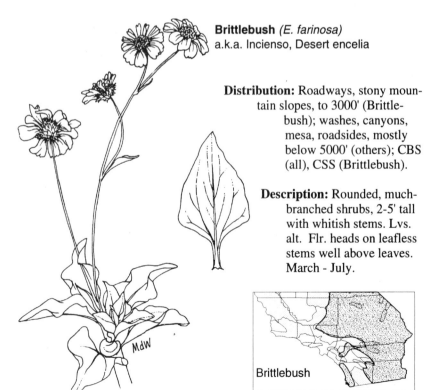

Brittlebush *(E. farinosa)*
a.k.a. Incienso, Desert encelia

Distribution: Roadways, stony mountain slopes, to 3000' (Brittlebush); washes, canyons, mesa, roadsides, mostly below 5000' (others); CBS (all), CSS (Brittlebush).

Description: Rounded, much-branched shrubs, 2-5' tall with whitish stems. Lvs. alt. Flr. heads on leafless stems well above leaves. March - July.

Brittlebush

94

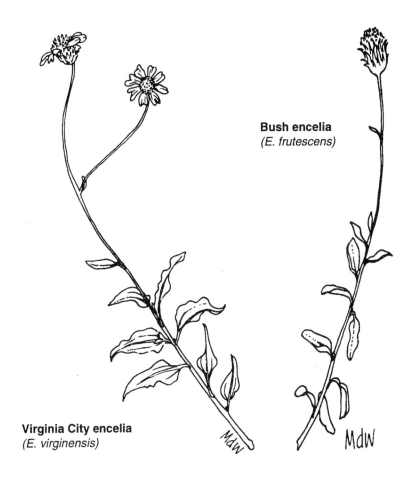

Bush encelia
(E. frutescens)

Virginia City encelia
(E. virginensis)

Notes: Brittlebush's gray-green leaves and bright yellow heads make it one of the most conspicuous shrubs of the rocky hillsides and roadways. Resin exuded from the stems was used by Indians as a glue and chewed as a treatment for many body aches. In Baja California the resin is burned in churches as incense, the origin of its alternate common name, incienso. Its leaves contain a chemical that washes into soil and prevents the growth of many other plants.

Another member of this group, California encelia (*E. californica*) is found in our coastal foothills. Brittlebush and Bush encelia commonly hybridize, creating much confusion in identification.

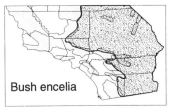

Bush encelia

95

Horsebrush *(Tetradymia)*

Sunflower Family (Asteraceae)

Key to species:

1   **A**—Branches armed with stout, rigid spines OR leaves spine-tipped; heads with 5 or more flowers; bracts below flower heads not keeled . Go to 2

    B—Branches unarmed and leaves not spine-tipped; heads 4-flowered; bracts below heads keeled . . . . Go to 4

2   **A**—Heads with five flowers . . . . . . **Mojave horsebrush** *(T. stenolepis)*

    B—Heads with six or more flowers . . . . Go to 3

3   **A**—Heads borne of short, axillary stalks (peduncles), each head with 6 or 7 flowers . . . . **Cotton-thorn** *(T. axillaris)*

    B—Heads not stalked, some heads with as many as 9 flowers . . . .
    . . . . **Hairy horsebrush** *(T. comosa)*

4   **A**—Mature leaves rarely exceeding 1/2" long, nearly hairless, and falling relatively soon . . . . **Little horsebrush** *(T. glabrata)*

    B—Leaves typically longer than 1/2", with white, woolly hairs, and remaining on plant . . . . **Gray horsebrush** *(T. canescens)*

Distribution: Mojave horsebrush, Little horsebrush and Cotton-thorn occur on dry slopes and flats of the Mojave Desert, from 2000 to 5000' (Mojave horsebrush) or 6500' (others); CBS, JTW, PJW. Gray Horsebrush occupies higher elevations (4000-8000') in the San Bernardino Mtns. and mtns. of Mojave Desert; SBS, PJW, YPF. Hairy horsebrush grows on coastal slopes and occasionally on the Mojave Desert below 5000'; CSS, Cha.

Gray horsebrush
(T. canescens)

MdW

Description: Horsebrushes are low, rigid shrubs, rarely exceeding 3-4' in height (1' for Gray). Branches (and usually leaves) are covered with a dense mat of woolly hairs. Lvs. alternate, simple, narrow, usually clustered, with smooth edges; in some species (see above) primary leaves are modified into stout spines. Flrs. yellow, all discoid, the ray flowers lacking. Involucral bracts 4-6, overlapping, often thickened at base. Apr.- May (Cotton-thorn), May - Aug. (Mojave, Little), July - Aug. (Gray), June - Sept. (Hairy).

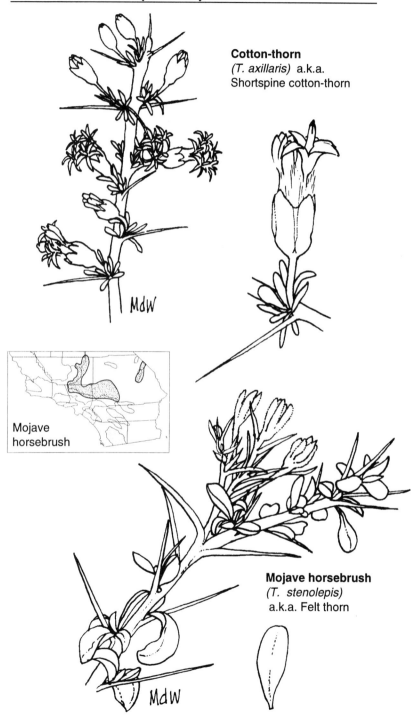

Cotton-thorn
(T. axillaris) a.k.a.
Shortspine cotton-thorn

MdW

Mojave
horsebrush

Mojave horsebrush
(T. stenolepis)
a.k.a. Felt thorn

MdW

Goldenhead *(Acamptopappus)*

Sunflower Family (Asteraceae)

Key to species:

1 | **A**—Heads lacking ray flowers . . . . . . **Goldenhead** *(A. sphaerocephalus)*
   | **B**—Heads with both ray and disc flowers . . . .
   | . . . .**Shockley goldenhead** *(A. shockleyi)*

Distribution: Open areas, below 6000' (Goldenhead) or up to 6700' (Shockley goldenhead); CBS, JTW.

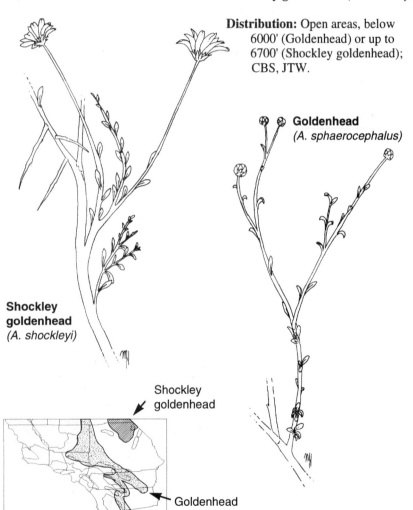

Goldenhead
(A. sphaerocephalus)

Shockley goldenhead
(A. shockleyi)

Shockley goldenhead

Goldenhead

Description: Small (to 1 1/2' tall), rounded shrubs with slender, white-barked, nearly hairless stems. Lvs. alt., simple, smooth-edged. Flr. heads more or less spherical, in loose clusters or solitary at ends of branches. Flrs. yellow. Bracts below flowering head broad, whitish, green-tipped, with dry, membranous, irregularly toothed edges. Apr. - June.

Sweet bush *(Bebbia juncea)*

a.k.a. Rush bebbia   Sunflower Family (Asteraceae)

Distribution: Gravelly washes, canyons below 4000'; CBS.

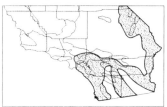

Description: Low (to 4' tall), rounded, strong-smelling bush with green, nearly leaf-less, many-branched stems. Lvs. opp. below, alt. above, simple, 1/4-2" long,less than 1/16" wide, the edges smooth or with 1 or 2 pairs of teeth near middle, falling after a brief period. Flr. heads in loose groups or solitary at ends of twigs. Flrs. yellow, discoid. Bracts below heads in several overlapping ranks, the inner ranks often reddish, the outer with fine grayish hairs. Apr. - July.

California trixis *(Trixis californica)*

Sunflower Family (Asteraceae)

Distribution: Below 3000' in sheltered canyons and stream-beds in the Colorado Desert and se. Mojave Desert; CBS.

Description: An erect, 1-3' tall shrub. Lvs. alt., simple, lance-shaped, 3/4 - 1 1/2" long, up to 5/8" wide; blade narrowing at base, petiole lacking, edge smooth or with a few shallow teeth. Heads in clusters or alone at ends of leafy branches, 9 - 12 flowered, all flrs. similar. Flrs. yellow, 1/2 - 3/4" long, with 2-lipped corollas, upper lip with 2 lobes, lower lip with 3. Bracts below heads leafy, the inner row straw-colored, 1/2" high. Fr. a slender, sticky achene. Feb. - April.

Burrobrush *(Hymenoclea salsola)*

a.k.a. Cheesebush   Sunflower Family (Asteraceae)

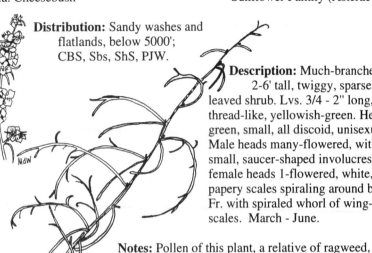

Distribution: Sandy washes and flatlands, below 5000'; CBS, Sbs, ShS, PJW.

Description: Much-branched, 2-6' tall, twiggy, sparsely-leaved shrub. Lvs. 3/4 - 2" long, thread-like, yellowish-green. Heads green, small, all discoid, unisexual. Male heads many-flowered, with small, saucer-shaped involucres; female heads 1-flowered, white, papery scales spiraling around base. Fr. with spiraled whorl of wing-like scales. March - June.

Notes: Pollen of this plant, a relative of ragweed, causes hay fever in some. When crushed, leaves emit a smell like that of cheese, hence its alternate name.

Related species: *H. monogyra*, might be mistaken for this species. It occurs near Needles and Rialto (San Bernardino Co.), and in Mission Valley in San Diego Co. Its bur has only a single whorl of bracts and it flowers in the autumn.

Desert sunflower *(Viguiera parishii)*

Sunflower Family (Asteraceae)

Distribution: Sandy canyons of eastern Mojave and Colorado Deserts; CBS, Cha, CSS.

Description: Rounded, much-branched, 1 - 2 1/2' tall shrub, basal branches with rough-feeling, sharp, stiff hairs. Lvs. opp., green, somewhat triangular, 1/2 - 1 1/4" long, with stiff, rough-feeling hairs. Heads yellow, solitary or in small clusters at ends of branch tips. Bracts beneath heads softly hairy, lance-shaped, in 2 - 3 ranks. Ray flrs. about 8, their ligules 1/2 - 5/8" long; disc flrs. numerous. Fr. a somewhat hairy achene. Feb.- June.

Desert sunflower (con't)

Related species: Another species of desert sunflower, *V. reticulata,* is occasionally found in the Mojave Desert. Its soft, hairy, ovalish rather than triangular leaves with strikingly raised veins on the underside distinguish it from its much more common cousin.

Pygmy-cedar *(Peucephyllum schottii)*
a.k.a. Desert Fir   Sunflower Family (Asteraceae)

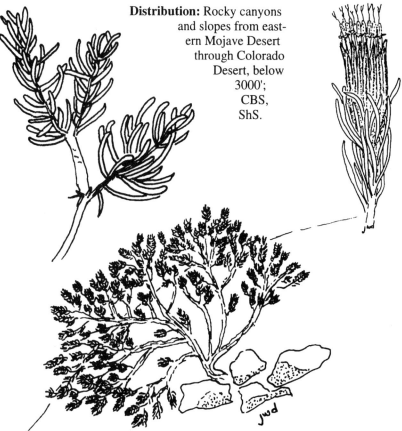

Distribution: Rocky canyons and slopes from eastern Mojave Desert through Colorado Desert, below 3000'; CBS, ShS.

Description: Erect, evergreen, aromatic, shrub, to 9' tall, often with trunk-like stem. Lvs. alt., needle-like, green, 1/4 - 1" long, with numerous dot-like glands, densely clustered at branch ends. Heads yellow, scattered and solitary, of disc flrs. only. Bracts beneath heads green, in 2 series, the outer long, narrow, round, the inner flattened. Fr. a hairy achene. Jan. - June.

Notes: The only desert-dwelling sunflower with dense, needle-form leaves, Pygmy-cedar is readily recognized. The balsam-like odor of the leaves is reminiscent of the smell of conifers.

Goldenbush *(Ericameria)*

Sunflower Family (Asteraceae)

Key to species:

1 | **A**—Most heads with 3 or fewer ray flowers, often with none . . . . . Go to 2
B—Most heads with 4 or more ray flowers . . . . .Go to 3

2 | **A**—Disc flowers mostly 9-20, occasionally more; leaves ovalish, 1/8 - 3/8" wide; plant grows from 4000 to 7500' on the desert side of our mountains . . . . **Wedgeleaf goldenbush** *(E. cuneata)*
B—Disc flowers mostly 5-9, often as many as 12; leaves less than 1/16" wide; plant from 2000 to 6000' from Little San Bernardino Mtns. northward across Mojave Desert . . . . . . **Cooper goldenbush** *(E. cooperi)*

3 | **A**—Involucre 1/4 - 5/8" wide . . . . Go to 4
B—Involucre typically less than 1/4" wide . . . . Go to 5

4 | **A**—Leaves threadlike, up to 1 1/2" long; corollas of ray flowers small, less than 1/4" long; plant barely enters Colorado Desert along western edge . . . . **Pine-bush** *(E. pinifolia)*
B—Leaves up to 1/8" wide, to 2" long; corollas of ray flowers exceeding 1/4" in length; plant widespread across Mojave Desert and western Colorado Desert . . . . **Interior goldenbush** *(E. linearifolia)*

5 | **A**—Leaves aromatic, hairless when young, to 1 1/4" long; ligules of ray flowers usually less than 1/8" long; plant 1-3' tall and grows above 3000' in the mountains of the Mojave Desert . . . . **Turpentine-brush** *(E. laricifolia)*
B—Leaves not particularly aromatic, finely haired when young, to 1 3/4" long; ligules of ray flowers 1/8 - 1/4" long; plant is 3 - 9' tall and grows below 2500' on the western edge of the Colorado desert . . . . **Palmer Goldenbush** *(E. palmeri)*

Description: Lvs. alt., simple, often gland-dotted. Flr. heads yellow. Involucre with numerous bracts, usually in 3-5 overlapping ranks. Ray flrs. fertile or sterile; disc flowers fertile. Fr. an achene. March - May (Interior) or June (Cooper); Aug. - Dec. (Palmer); Sept. - Oct. (Turpentine-brush) or Nov. (Wedgeleaf).

Wedgeleaf goldenbush
(E. cuneata)

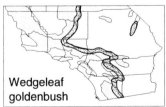

Wedgeleaf
goldenbush

Goldenbush (con't)

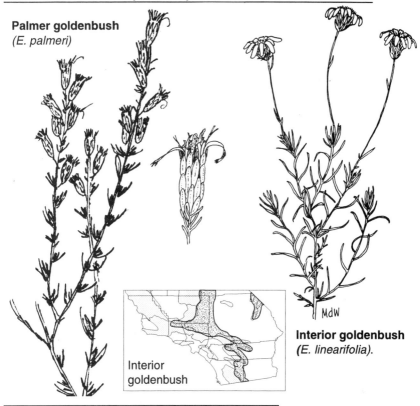

Palmer goldenbush
(E. palmeri)

Interior goldenbush
(E. linearifolia).

Interior
goldenbush

MdW

Pale-leaf goldenbush *(Isocoma acradenia)*
Sunflower Family (Asteraceae)

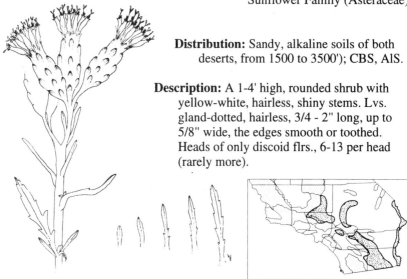

Distribution: Sandy, alkaline soils of both
deserts, from 1500 to 3500'); CBS, AlS.

Description: A 1-4' high, rounded shrub with
yellow-white, hairless, shiny stems. Lvs.
gland-dotted, hairless, 3/4 - 2" long, up to
5/8" wide, the edges smooth or toothed.
Heads of only discoid flrs., 6-13 per head
(rarely more).

Sagebrush *(Artemisia)*

a.k.a. Wormwood   Sunflower Family (Asteraceae)

Key to species:

1 | A—Plant with spines, the remnants of flowering stalks when the heads fall; inflorescences short, the flowering heads mostly hidden by leaves; flowering in spring or early summer; branches and leaves with a dense mat of white hair; plant grows from 2000 to 6000' in western Mojave Desert . . . . **Budsage** *(A. spinescens)*
B—Plant not spiny; inflorescences on long stalks mostly well above leaves; flowering in late summer to fall; branches and leaves not densely white-hairy . . . . .Go to 2

2 | A—Plant typically taller than 2' (often to 15'), with a definite trunk; plant grows on desert-facing slopes of mountains on western side of Mojave Desert, 1000 to 10,000' . . . . **Big sagebrush** *(A. tridentata)*
B—Plant 2' or less tall, without a distinctive trunk . . . . Go to 3

3 | A—Disc flowers number 10-16; leaves up to 2" long, broadly wedge- or fan-shaped, the apex 3-lobed; plant grows on rocky slopes on the north face of San Bernardino Mtns, 2500 - 11,000 . . . . **Rothrock sagebrush** *(A. rothrockii)*
B—Disc flowers 5 or fewer; leaves mostly less than 3/4" long . . . . Go to 4

4 | A—Ray flowers absent; disc flowers 3-5; plant occurs from 5000 to 11,000' on desert-facing slopes of San Bernardino Mtns., in Hemet Valley (San Jacinto Mtns.) or in mtns. of eastern Mojave Desert . . . . **Black sagebrush** *(A. nova)*
B—Ray flowers typically 1 or 2 (rarely 0); disc flowers do not exceed 3 in number; plant occurs form 5000-6000' in Clark or New York Mtns. in eastern Mojave Desert . . . . **Bigelow sagebrush** *(A. bigelovii)*

Distribution: Although typical of desert foothills along the western side of our deserts Big sagebrush also ranges across the San Gabriel Mtns. almost to the coast in the Sta. Clara River basin, Ventura Co.; SBS, YPF, Cha, PJW, JTW. Budsage; ShS, CBS. Black sagebrush; SBS, PJW, YPF. Rothrock and Bigelow sagebrush; PJW.

Description: Mostly gray, strongly aromatic, densely branched shrubs. Lvs. usually wedge-shaped, widening towards apex, and ending in three (rarely 5 or 7) lobes or teeth, densely covered with fine hairs. Heads usually numerous, inconspicuous, in panicles. Fr. an achene. Mar. - June (Budsage), July - Dec. (Big), Aug.- Sept. (Rothrock), Sept. - Nov. (Bigelow, Black).

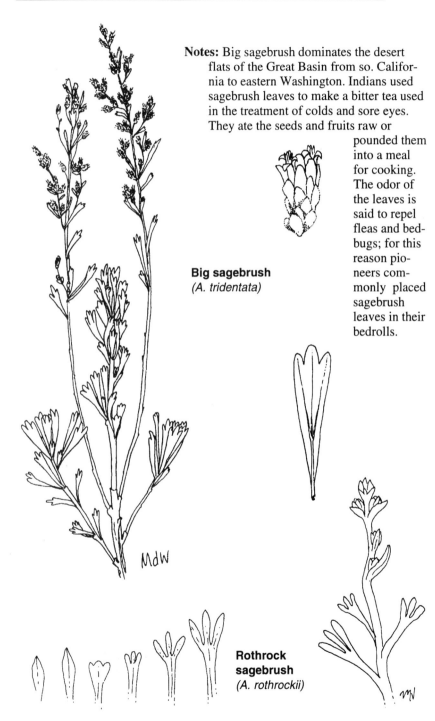

Notes: Big sagebrush dominates the desert flats of the Great Basin from so. California to eastern Washington. Indians used sagebrush leaves to make a bitter tea used in the treatment of colds and sore eyes. They ate the seeds and fruits raw or pounded them into a meal for cooking. The odor of the leaves is said to repel fleas and bedbugs; for this reason pioneers commonly placed sagebrush leaves in their bedrolls.

Big sagebrush
(A. tridentata)

MdW

Rothrock sagebrush
(A. rothrockii)

105

Rabbitbrush *(Chrysothamnus)*

Sunflower Family (Asteraceae)

Key to species:

1 **A**—Leaves almost round in cross section, dotted with depressed resin glands, sticky . . . . Go to 2
B—Leaves generally flattened, not gland-dotted, usually not sticky (Yellow rabbitbrush is an exception) . . . . Go to 3

2 **A**—Stems with occasional black bands (a fungus); tips of bracts beneath heads not swollen and glandular; heads on stalks, abundant, occurring singly or in 2s or 3s; plant occurs below 4000' on western or northern boundaries of Colorado Desert or in the Mojave Desert . . . . **Black-stem rabbitbrush** *(C. paniculatus)*
B—Stems without black bands; tips of bracts below heads swollen and glandular; heads not on stalks, relatively few on each twig, in short racemes at the branch ends; plant occurs above 3200' on east-facing slopes of Santa Rosa Mountains or on the western or northern edges of the Mojave Desert . . . . **Roundleaf rabbitbrush** *(C. teretifolius)*

3 **A**—Leaves not twisted, covered with a dense felt-like mat of gray-green to whitish hairs; plant occurs above 2500' on the desert-fringing slopes on western side of the Colorado Desert and throughout Mojave Desert . . . . **Rubber rabbitbrush** *(C. nauseosus)*
B—Leaves twisted, hairless or only slightly hairy; plant occurs on the desert-facing slopes on west side of both deserts, mostly above 4000' . . . . **Yellow rabbitbrush** *(C. viscidiflorus)*

Distribution: Black-stem rabbitbrush: CBS. Roundleaf rabbitbrush: SbS, CBS, JTW, PJW. Rubber rabbitbrush: AlS, CBS, JTW, SbS, YPF. Yellow rabbitbrush: SbS, PFW, YPF.

MdW Rubber rabbitbrush *(C. nauseosus)*

Description: Much-branched shrubs, stems erect, broom-like, to 2' (Yellow) or 3-4' high (others). Lvs. alt., thread-like, smooth-edged, not clustered, up to 1" (Roundleaf), 1 1/2" (Black-stem, Yellow) or 2 1/2" (Rubber) long, less than 1/16" wide. Heads yellow, mostly 5-flowered, disc flowers only, in clusters at branch ends. Involucres less than 1/4" tall (Black-stem, Yellow), up to 3/8" (Roundleaf) and 1/2" (Rubber). Fr. an achene with soft, white bristles. June-Dec (Black-stem), Aug. - Oct. (Rubber), Sept.-Nov. (Roundleaf, Yellow).

Rabbitbrush (con't)

Notes: Though common, the rabbit-brushes are scarcely noticed except when in bloom. Rubber rabbitbrush, the most wide-ranging of our species, is also highly variable; botanists recognize eight distinctive subspecies based largely on degree of hairiness of leaves and achene. It is particularly common on deteriorated rangeland and along roadsides. Its English name derives from its rubbery sap, its latin name (nauseosus) from its rank, nausea-inducing smell.

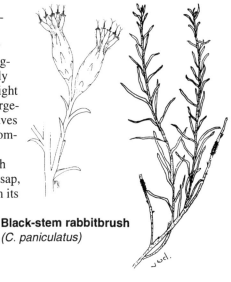

Black-stem rabbitbrush
(C. paniculatus)

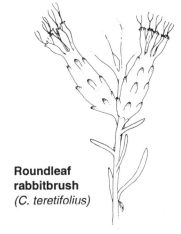

Roundleaf rabbitbrush
(C. teretifolius)

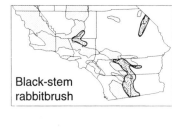

Black-stem rabbitbrush

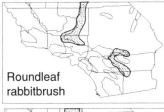

Roundleaf rabbitbrush

Yellow rabbitbrush

Yellow rabbitbrush
(C. viscidiflorus)

Brickellbush *(Brickellia)*

Sunflower Family (Asteraceae)

Key to species:

1 | A—Flowering heads 3/8" or more long, solitary at branch tips . . . Go to 2
   | B—Heads less than 3/8" long, in clusters at branch tips . . . . Go to 5

2 | A—Leaf edges are sharply toothed; leaves have short, but distinct petiole; below 3600' in eastern Mojave and w. Colorado Deserts . . . . **Pungent brickellbush** *(B. arguta)*
   | B—Leaf edges smooth; leaves nearly without petiole . . . . Go to 3

3 | A—Heads of about 60 flowers, more than 1" across when in fruit; bracts below heads densely woolly; uncommon, below 4000' in both deserts . . . . **White brickellbush** *(B. incana)*
   | B—Heads with 50 or fewer flowers, 1/2" or less across when in fruit; bracts not densely woolly . . . . Go to 4

4 | A—Heads with 40-50 flowers; leaves often exceed 1/2" in length; leaves and twigs covered with a short, scarcely noticeable hairs; common, western edge of Moj. & no. Colo. Des. . **Mojave brickellbush** *(B. oblongifolia)*
   | B—Heads with fewer than 35 flowers; leaves not more than 3/8" long; branches spiny, both twigs and leaves covered with long, twisted hairs; Colo. Des., 2000 - 4000' . . . . **Rigid brickellbush** *(B. frutescens)*

5 | A—Heads of more than 8 flowers and 1/2" or more long . . . . . . Go to 6
   | B—Heads of fewer than 8 flowers, rarely exceeding 3/8" in length; uncommon plant of northern Mojave Desert . . . . **Inyo brickellbush** *(B. multiflora)* [but see comment on related species]

6 | A—Tips of bracts below heads turn out and down; leaves almost petioleless; uncommon, Mojave Des. . . . **Littleleaf brickellbush** *(B. microphylla)*
   | B—Tips of the involucral bracts erect, not spreading; leaves with short but distinct petiole, usually longer than 1/8" . . . . Go to 7

7 | A— Bracts beneath heads covered with fine hairs; common, western Colorado Desert . . . . **Desert brickellbush** *(B. desertorum)*
   | B—Bracts beneath heads hairless or nearly so; common, western edges of both deserts . . . . **California brickellbush** *(B. californica)*

Related species: A rare form of brickellbush, **Knapp's** *(B. knappiana),* occurs in the Kingston and Panamint Mtns. of the eastern Mojave Desert and might be confused with this species. It differs from Inyo brickellbush in that its involucral bracts are downy hairy, its leaves are longer, their edges sawtoothed. Though given its own species name, the plant may be a hybrid between Inyo brickellbush and either California or Desert brickellbush.

Distribution: Sandy washes, flats, rocky places. Pungent, Mojave, Littleleaf, Inyo; CBS JTW, PJW. Desert, Rigid; CBS, PJW. White; CBS, JTW, ShS.

Brickellbush (con't)

Description: Small shrubs or subshrubs with simple, mostly resin-dotted leaves. Flrs. discoid, whitish or tinged with green or purple. Fr. a 10-ribbed achene. April - May (Pungent), June (Rigid, Mojave) or Oct (White); Aug -Nov. (Desert, Littleleaf, Inyo).

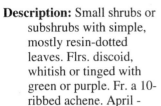
Mojave brickellbush

Notes: Most brickellbushes barely qualify as shrubs, but all have woody stems. Most are easily overlooked and some are quite uncommon.

Mojave brickellbush
(B. oblongifolia)

White brickellbush
(B. incana)

fruiting heads

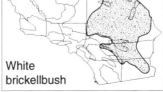
White brickellbush

Pungent brickellbush
(B. arguta)

Baccharis *(Baccharis)*

Sunflower Family (Asteraceae)

Key to species:

1 | A—Branches woody well above base; mature leaves longer than 3/4" . . . .
. . . . Go to 2
B—Branches herbaceous, the only woody portion the base of the plant itself; mature leaves mostly less than 3/4" long, few, the upper ones scalelike; plant of dry washes in w. Colorado Desert or near Joshua Tree National Monument . . . . **Shortleaf baccharis** *(B. brachyphylla)*

2 | A—Branches broomlike (i.e., narrow, numerous, clustered in nearly parallel groups), with distinct longitudinal furrows or ridges; plant almost leafless, dropping most of its leaves before the flowers open . . Go to 3
B—Branches not broomlike, with or without longitudinal furrows or ridges; plant leafy all year . . . . Go to 4

3 | A—Larger leaves narrowly linear, rigid, up to 2" long; plant of sandy washes of Colorado Desert, below 1200' . . **Broom baccharis** *(B. sarothroides)*
B—Larger leaves wider towards tip than at base, rarely exceeding 1" in length; plant of canyon bottoms in both deserts, below 4500' . . . .
. . . . **Squaw waterweed** *(B. sergiloides)*

4 | A—Leaves 1-6" long, narrow, willow-like, mostly 3-veined from the base, the edges smooth or with evenly spaced teeth all around; flower heads grow at tips of main branches or on short lateral branches;plant grows along watercourses throughout Colorado Desert and in eastern Mojave Desert, below 3500' . . . . . . **Mule fat** or **Seep willow** *(B. salicifolia)*
B—Leaves 3/4 - 1 1/2" long, wedge-shaped, broadest above middle, the edges smooth or few-toothed above the middle; flower heads on almost leafless stalks; plant grows along streams in the Colorado and northern. Mojave Deserts, below 2000' . . . . . . **Emory baccharis** *(B. emoryi)*

Distribution: CSS, Cha, CBS (all), PJW (Squaw waterweed).

Description: Shrubs, twigs and lvs. often sticky. Lvs. alt., simple. Flr. heads white or yellowish, all disc, male and female flrs. on separate plants. Bracts below heads whitish, papery, in overlapping rows. Fr. an achene with long, white bristles.

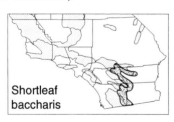

Shortleaf baccharis

Notes: Because of its similar leaf form and its stream-side habitat, Mule fat is frequently mistaken for willow. Its compound floral heads quickly separates it from the catkin-bearing willows. Livestock often forage on it, hence its name.

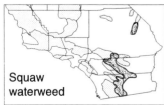

Squaw waterweed

Baccharis (con't)

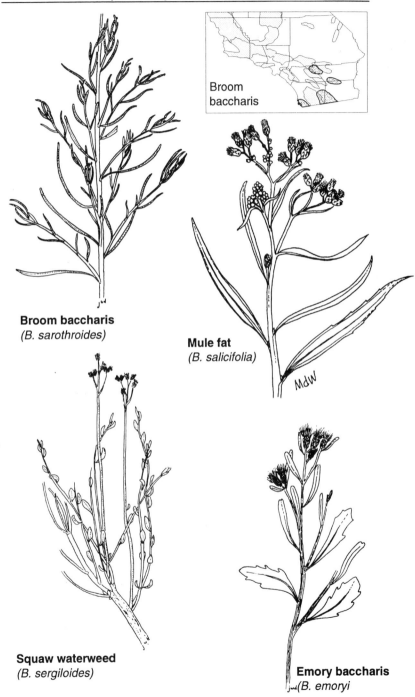

Broom
baccharis

Broom baccharis
(B. sarothroides)

Mule fat
(B. salicifolia)

Squaw waterweed
(B. sergiloides)

Emory baccharis
(B. emoryi

Arrow weed *(Pluchea sericea)*

Sunflower Family (Asteraceae)

Distribution: River bottoms, ditches, wet places throughout both deserts to the Colorado River where it is abundant; CSS, CBS, others.

Description: Willow-like shrub, 3-12' tall, with straight slender stems. Lvs. simple, alt., 3/4 - 1 1/2" long, 1/8 - 1/4" wide, lance-shaped; blade tapering to a petiole-like base, edge smooth. Heads purplish, clustered, of disc flrs. only; central flrs. with 5-toothed corollas. Involucral bracts in 2-3 ranks, softly hairy, outer ones broad, brown to purplish, inner ones narrower, whitish. Fr. a grooved achene. March - July.

Notes: This is our only blue-flowered, shrubby member of the sunflower family. Its English name derives from the use of its straight stems for arrow making by Indians.

Related species: Though superficially resembling willows both in leaf shape and habitat, Arrowweed's purple sunflower-like heads distinguish it.

Arrow-leaf *(Pleurocoronis pluriseta)*

Sunflower Family (Asteraceae)

Distribution: Rocky soils in both deserts below 4000'; CBS.

Description: A low, rounded shrub, 1-2' tall, with white shredding bark on older stems. Lvs. simple, the upper alt., lower opp. Blade triangular to lance-shaped, less than 3/8" long, the edges smooth or with a 2-4 small teeth; petiole several times longer than blade, 3/4 - 1 1/2". Heads few, in small clusters at branch tips, underlain by several series of involucral bracts, each bract marked with 3 fine lines, the inner bracts lance-shaped, the outer oval. Flrs. whitish, all disc, about 20 per head; stigmas purplish at tip. April - May.

Golden-yarrow *(Eriophyllum confertiflorum)*

Sunflower Family (Asteraceae)

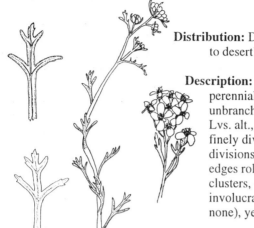

Distribution: Dry slopes, canyons from coast to desert's edge; Cha, CSS, others.

Description: Shrubby, slender-stemmed perennial, woody at base, stems mostly unbranched, covered with white wool. Lvs. alt., simple, 3/4–1 1/4" long, finely divided into narrow, thread-like divisions, white woolly beneath, the edges rolled under. Heads in small clusters, each head with 4–7 oval involucral bracts. Ray flrs. 4–6 (or none), yellow.

Related Species: This is a highly plastic species, with many variants, including one that lacks ray flowers.

Bush groundsel *(Senecio flaccidus)*

a.k.a. Bush senecio, Shrubby butterweed   Sunflower Family (Asteraceae)

Distribution: Dry stream beds of Mojave and n. Colorado Deserts, below 6000'; Cha CSS, FhW, VGr, CBS, PJW.

Description: Much-branched, bushy shrub, 2–5' tall, stems densely long-hairy with fine lines or grooves. Lvs. alt., 1–4" long, divided pinnately into 3–9 thread-like lobes, hairless and gray-green above, white-hairy or hairless beneath; smaller lvs. in axil of larger. Ray and disc flrs. yellow, in loosely branching clusters; rays 10–13, showy, 1/2" long. Involucres with single row of long, uniform bracts, a row of shorter, spreading bractlets at the base. Fr. a hairy achene. June–Oct.; March–May in deserts.

Related species: Sixteen non-woody Senecios occur in so. Calif.; the genus is easily recognized by the single rank of tall involucral bracts.

Notes: All Senecios are toxic to livestock and probably to humans. Consumption causes liver failure and damage to the nervous system.

Matchweed *(Gutierrezia)*

Sunflower Family (Asteraceae)

Key to species:

1 **A**—Heads very small, less than 1/8" high, usually with one ray and one disc flower (rarely 2 of each); 2 main and 2 or 3 shorter bracts beneath each head, the longer main bract enveloping the ray flower, the shorter enclosing the disk flower, the bracts leathery, yellowish with papery edges and warty tips; plant of western and northern Mojave Desert, 2000-7500' . . . . **Sticky matchweed** (*G. microcephala*)

  B—Heads about 1/4" high, with 4 - 8 ray, 3 - 10 disk flowers; several main bracts beneath each head, thickened at tips; plant of desert-facing slopes of San Gabriel, San Bernardino, San Jacinto, Sta. Rosa Mtns, and mtns. of e. Mojave Desert, to 10,000' . . . **Broom matchweed** (*G. sarothrae*)

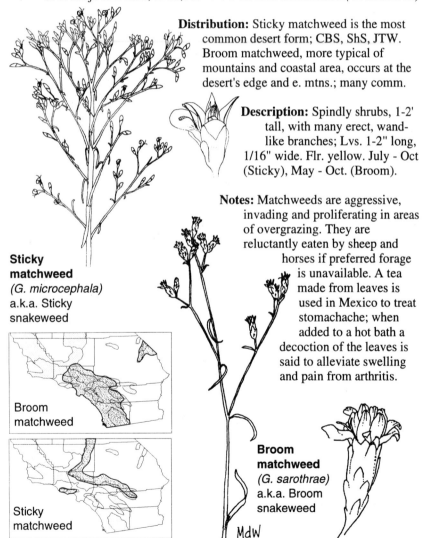

Distribution: Sticky matchweed is the most common desert form; CBS, ShS, JTW. Broom matchweed, more typical of mountains and coastal area, occurs at the desert's edge and e. mtns.; many comm.

Description: Spindly shrubs, 1-2' tall, with many erect, wand-like branches; Lvs. 1-2" long, 1/16" wide. Flr. yellow. July - Oct (Sticky), May - Oct. (Broom).

Notes: Matchweeds are aggressive, invading and proliferating in areas of overgrazing. They are reluctantly eaten by sheep and horses if preferred forage is unavailable. A tea made from leaves is used in Mexico to treat stomachache; when added to a hot bath a decoction of the leaves is said to alleviate swelling and pain from arthritis.

Sticky matchweed
(G. microcephala)
a.k.a. Sticky snakeweed

Broom matchweed

Sticky matchweed

Broom matchweed
(G. sarothrae)
a.k.a. Broom snakeweed

MdW

Scale- & Green-broom *(Lepidospartum)*

Sunflower Family (Asteraceae)

Key to species:

1   **A**—Leaves below heads about 1/8" long, scale-like; 10+ flowers per head; common on west edge of both deserts . . **Scale-broom** *(L. squamatum)*

    B—Leaves below heads 1" or more long, thread-like; 5 flowers per head;San Gabriel and Clark Mtns. . . . . **Green-broom** *(L. latisquamum)*

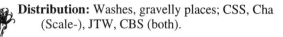

Distribution: Washes, gravelly places; CSS, Cha (Scale-), JTW, CBS (both).

Description: Rigid, broom-like, nearly leafless shrubs, to 6' tall. Stems wand-like, younger white-hairy, older hairless. Lvs. alt., scale-like, to 3/8" long (Scale-) or thread-like (Green-). Heads numerous, clustered at branch ends. Flrs. discoid, yellow, with long corolla tube, long lobes. Bracts below heads papery, in 3-4 rows. Fr. a cottony achene. June - Dec.

MdW

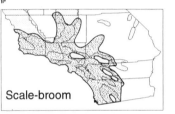

Scale-broom

Calif. buckwheat *(Eriogonum fasciculatum)*

Buckwheat Family (Polygonaceae)

Distribution: Abundant on hillsides, washes, roadways, 1000-7000'; CSS, CBS, Cha, PJW, SbS.

Description: Low, spreading shrub, to 3' tall. Lvs. alt., simple, less than 3/4" long, 1/4" wide, edges smooth and rolled under, in tight clusters. Flrs. small, in tight clusters underlain by leafy bracts, well above plant's leafy portion on a branched, leafless stalk: Se. 6, white or pinkish, united at base; Pe. none; St. 9; Ov. sup., 1-celled. Fr. a 3-angled achene. April - Oct.

Notes: Common shrub throughout s. Calif., from coast to desert edge. The species is highly variable. The most common desert form, var. *polifolium,* differs from the coastal variety in having hairy leaves and calyces. Bees foraging on the plant produce a high quality honey. Dried flowers persist most of the year in reddish-brown heads. The seeds are probably edible but hardly worth the effort. Commercial buckwheat flour comes from a relative, *Pagopyrum..*

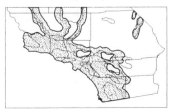

Flannel bush *(Fremontodendron californicum)*

a.k.a. Fremontia,
Calif. slippery elm

Cacao Family (Sterculiaceae)

Distribution: Dry, granitic slopes, 3000-7000';
Cha, YPF, PJW.

Description: Spreading, shrub, 10-20' tall,
evergreen but dropping leaves during drought.
Lvs. alt., simple, palmately 3- to 5-lobed, on
short spurs; blade dull green, covered with
star-shaped, tawny, matted wool, densest
below. Flrs. 1 1/2 - 2 1/2" across:
Se. showy, petal-like, yellow,
basal glands long-haired; Pe.
none; St. 5, filaments joined; Ov.
sup., 4- to 5-celled, surrounded by
filament tube, style extending past
anthers. Fr. a bristly capsule, 3/4 -
1" long. May - June.

Notes: Because of its attractive flowers, the
showy yellow sepals masking as petals,
Flannel bush is widely used as an
ornamental. A tea from the leaves is said to be an
excellent expectorant and soothing to sore throats.

Related species: The rare **Mexican flannel bush** *(F. mexicanum)* is seen
occasionally in San Diego Co. near the Mexican border. It is distinguished
from its more common cousin by the lack of hair on the glands at the base
of the sepals, and by its larger flowers, 2 1/2 - 4" across.

Jojoba *(Simmondsia chinensis)*

a.k.a. Goatnut, Deernut, Pignut,
Sheepnut, Lemonleaf, Quinine plant,
Wild hazel, Coffeebush

Jojoba Family (Simmonsiaceae)

Distribution: Dry, rocky slopes, below
5000'; CBS , JTW, Cha.

Description: A 3-9' tall, gray-green or
yellowish spreading shrub. Lvs. 1-2"
long, opp., simple, leathery, minutely hairy on both sides;
edges smooth; petiole less than 1/16". Flrs. without petals,
unisexual, male and female flrs. on separate plants. Male
flrs. in short, head-like clusters: Se. 5, distinct; St.10-12.
Female flrs. solitary on short peduncles: Se. 5, unequal, growing as fruit
develops; Ov. sup., 3-celled. Fr. smooth, round, thick-walled capsule,
partially enclosed by sepals. March-May.

Jojoba (con't)

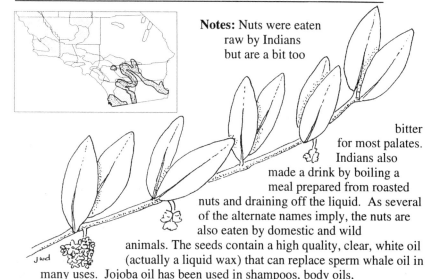

Notes: Nuts were eaten raw by Indians but are a bit too bitter for most palates. Indians also made a drink by boiling a meal prepared from roasted nuts and draining off the liquid. As several of the alternate names imply, the nuts are also eaten by domestic and wild animals. The seeds contain a high quality, clear, white oil (actually a liquid wax) that can replace sperm whale oil in many uses. Jojoba oil has been used in shampoos, body oils, pharmaceuticals, cosmetics and as a hair restorer, though it probably did little more than put a shine on many bald heads.

Castor bean *(Ricinus communis)*

a.k.a. Palma Christi · Spurge Family (Euphorbiaceae)

Distribution: A non-native, castor bean has been naturalized throughout so. California. It is found, often in abundance, in disturbed areas.

Description: Red-stemmed, tree-like, shrub, 3-10' tall, with palmately lobed leaves. Lvs. alt., 4-16" broad, 5- to 11-lobed, lobes toothed; petiole attached to lower surface, not edge, of leaf. Flrs. in clusters, unisexual, greenish, male flrs. below female. Ca. 3- to 5-parted; Pe. none; St. many, with branched filaments; Ov. sup., 3-celled, with 3 feather-like, red styles. Fr. a soft, spiny capsule, 3/8-1" thick. Seeds shiny, mottled. Flowers most of year.

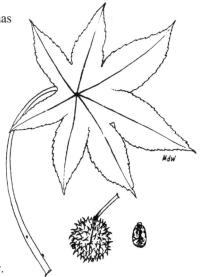

Notes: This plant is the source of castor oil, long used as a laxative, lubricant, and in soap manufacture. Seeds and leaves are toxic if eaten. Ricin, one of the most toxic substances known, is released when the seeds are crushed. A sublethal dose of seeds causes vomiting, diarrhea and convulsions.

Saltbushes *(Atriplex)*

Goosefoot Family (Chenopodiaceae)

Key to species:

1 A—Tips of branches distinctly sharp-pointed and spine-like . . . . . Go to 2
   B—Tips of branches generally not sharp-tipped or spine-like . . . . Go to 5

2 A—Base of leaves distinctly heart-shaped; fruiting bracts thickish, fanshaped, broader at top than at base . . . . **Parry saltbush** *(A. parryi)*
   B—Base of leave not heart-shaped; fruiting bracts not as above . . . Go to 3

3 A—Leaf blade round or oval; fruiting bracts round or elliptical, with smooth edges . . . . **Shadscale** *(A. confertifolia)*
   B—Leaf blade more or less arrow-shape, broadest near base and tapering to a blunt point; top edges of fruiting bracts toothed or smooth . . . Go to 4

4 A—Fruiting bracts swollen at base, their top edges coarsely toothed wings; leaf blade rarely longer than 1" . . . . **Spinescale** *(A. spinifera)*
   B—Fruiting bracts flattened with smooth or faintly toothed edges, circular in outline or slightly broader than long; leaf blades sometimes reaching 1 1/2" . . . . **Big saltbush** *(A. lentiformis)*

5 A—leaves coarsely toothed, holly-like; fruiting bracts smooth-edged, flat, and circular in outline . . . . **Desert holly** *(A. hymenelytra)*
   B—Leaves smooth edged; edges of fruiting bracts usually at least faintly toothed, but sometimes smooth . . . . Go to 6

6 A—Leaves not exceeding 3/4" in length, in clusters when small; fruiting bracts fused, not much flattened, with thin, toothed edges and faces fringed with short tubercles . . . . **Allscale** *(A. polycarpa)*
   B—Leaves often 1" or more long, not clustered; fruiting bracts not as above . . . . Go to 7

7 A—Leaves up to 2" long; bracts around fruit (and female flowers) hard with four obvious longitudinal wings . . **Fourwing saltbush** *(A. canescens)*
   B—Leaves up to 1 1/2" long; fruiting bracts flattened with smooth or faintly toothed edges, circular or slightly broader than long . . . . **Big saltbush** *(A. lentiformis)*

Distribution: Saline soils. Fourwing saltbush occurs in both deserts to 7000'; AlS, CBS, PJW, JTW, CSS. Big saltbush, to 2000'; AlS, CSS, CSM. Desert holly, Allscale occupy both deserts, below 5000'; CBS, AlS. Parry saltbush, Shadscale, Spinescale occur only in the Mojave Desert (the latter two only in the western part), to 4000', 7000' and 2500', respectively; AlS, CBS.

Saltbushes (con't)

Description: Fourwing saltbush, Allscale, Big saltbush, and Spinescale commonly reach heights of 5' or more; Desert holly and Shadscale rarely exceed 3', Perry Saltbush 1'. Leaf surfaces are scurfy (covered with gray or white bran-like hairs). Flrs. lack petals, male and female flrs. on separate plants. Male flrs. bractless; Ca. 3-5 lobed, St. 3-5. Female flrs. (and fruit) with 2 leaf-like bracts; Ov. 1-celled, 2-styled.

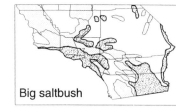

Big saltbush

Big saltbush
(A. lentiformis)
a.k.a. Lenscale,
Quail brush

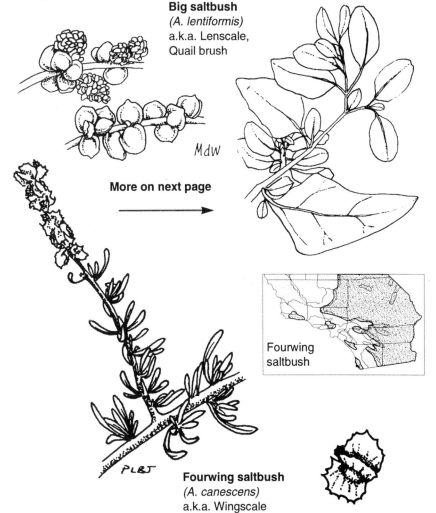

MdW

More on next page

→

Fourwing
saltbush

PLBJ

Fourwing saltbush
(A. canescens)
a.k.a. Wingscale

Saltbushes (con't)

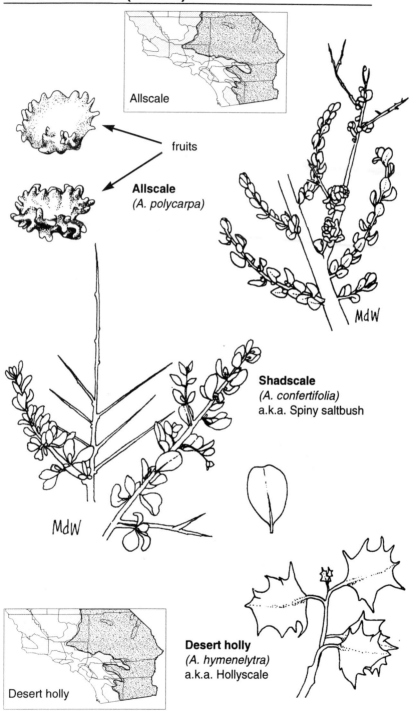

Allscale

fruits

Allscale
(A. polycarpa)

MdW

Shadscale
(A. confertifolia)
a.k.a. Spiny saltbush

MdW

Desert holly
(A. hymenelytra)
a.k.a. Hollyscale

Desert holly

Hop-sage *(Grayia spinosa)*

Goosefoot Family (Chenopodiaceae)

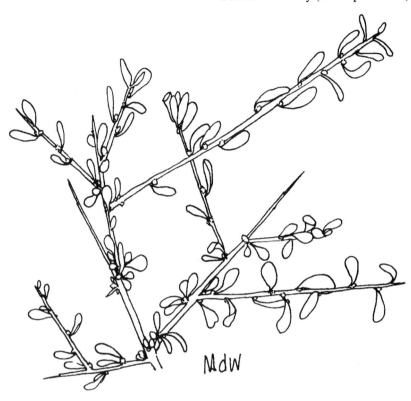

Distribution: Common in alkaline flats of Mojave Desert, rare on w. Colorado Desert, from 2500-7500'; CBS, JTW, PJW.

Description: A low (1-3' tall), diffusely branched, shrub with spiny twigs and mealy younger parts. Lvs. alternate, simple, gray-green, somewhat fleshy, 1/2-1 1/2" long, more or less lance-shaped, with smooth edges. Flrs. small, greenish, male and female flowers separate on same or different plants, in dense spike-like clusters at ends of branches. Male flrs: Se. 4- (or 5-) parted; Pe. none; St. 4-5. Female flrs: Se. none; Pe. none; Ov. almost enclosed by pair of flat, membranous, red to whitish bracts, the bracts united almost to the top, notched at apex, and folded along the midrib. Fr. 1/4-1/2" wide, encased in bracts, with thin, membranous wings. March-June.

Notes: This plant occurs in alkaline soils, together with saltbushes and other members of the goosefoot family. It differs from saltbushes in having entirely joined fruiting bracts; even so, some botanists would place it in the genus *Atriplex,* with the saltbushes.

Winter fat *(Krascheninnikovia lanata)*

a.k.a. Lamb's tail   Goosefoot Family (Chenopodiaceae)

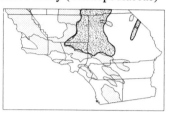

Distribution: Mesas, flats of Mojave Desert, 2000-7000'; CBS, JTW, PJW.

Description: Slender-branched, 1-3' tall, erect shrub, densely covered with white to rusty-colored, star-shaped or unbranched hairs, the stems somewhat spine-tipped.

Lvs. alt., simple, long and narrow, lacking petioles, often clustered, to 1 3/4" long, the edges smooth, rolled under. Flrs. in dense panicles among upper branches, male and female flrs. separate on same or different plant. Male flrs. bractless: Se. 4; Pe. none; St. 4, opposite sepals. Female flrs. with 2 densely hairy bracts, united to top: Se. none; Pe. none; Ov. sup., 2-celled, 2-styled. Fr. 1/4" long, 2-beaked, enclosed in membranous sac (bracts) densely covered with long, silvery hairs. March-August.

Notes: Livestock eat plant in winter when other forage is scarce, hence its name. Its alternate name, lamb's tail, derives from the distinctive rows of cottony fruits.

Iodine bush *(Allenrolfea occidentalis)*

a.k.a. Bush pickleweed   Goosefoot Family (Chenopodiaceae)

Distribution: Alkaline flats, salt lakes, other moist, saline places in both deserts; AlS.

Description: Succulent, 2-4' high, many-branched, apparently leafless shrub. Stems a series of short, cylindrical, hairless joints; greenish to pinkish when young, dark brown when older. Lvs. tiny, triangular, scales. Flrs. minute, 3-5 in axils of fleshy bracts, arranged spirally in cylindrical, 1/4 - 1" long spikes at ends of branches. Ca. 4- or 5-lobed, angled. Pe. none. St. 1-2, slightly extending beyond perianth; Ov. sup, 1-celled, with 2 (rarely 3) styles. Fr. ovoid, encased in calyx. June - Aug.

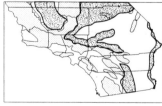

Notes: Iodine bush is more salt tolerant than any other shrub. Crushed stems leave a dark stain on the fingers, the source of plant's common name.

Bush seepweed *(Suaeda moquinii)*

a.k.a. Desert blite, Ink weed   Goosefoot Family (Chenopodiaceae)

Distribution: Alkali and salt flats throughout both deserts; CBS, AlS, CSS, CSM.

Description: A 1-3' high, sparsely leafy subshrub, woody at base, with slender, ascending branches. Lvs. alt., linear, 5/8 - 1 1/2" long, fleshy and succulent, green, without petioles. Flrs. small, greenish, 1 to 4 together in axils of leaves: Ca. fleshy, 5-lobed, lobes longer than undivided part of calyx; Pe. none; St. 5; Ov. sup., 1-celled, with 2 stigmas. May-Sept.

Notes: "Blite," the plant's alternate name, derives from a Latin word meaning "insipid" or lacking in desirable taste. Those who have tried the plant raw report the name to be quite apt! Boiled and rinsed of its salt, however, seepweed is a palatable addition to soup or salad. A black dye is derived from this and related species and for this reason all are sometimes called Ink weed. Indians found the dye useful in basket making and hair coloring. Early inhabitants of San Diego used the ashes of the plant in soap making.

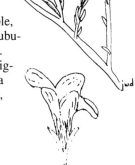

Greenfire *(Menodora spinescens)*

a.k.a. Spiny menodora, Ground thorn   Olive Family (Olivaceae)

Distribution: Canyons, rocky slopes and mesas of eastern Mojave Desert Mtns., n. slope of San Bernardino Mtn., and near Barstow, 2800-5000'; SsS CBS, JTW.

Description: A 1-3' tall, intricately-branched shrub, its stems short, stout, yellow-green, spine-tipped, covered with fine hairs. Lvs. alt., simple, fleshy, to 1/2" long, smooth-edged, without petiole. Flrs. white to faintly purple, regular. Ca. 5-7 narrow, rough-hairy lobes; Co. tubular, to 1/4" long, with 4-6 flaring lobes; St. 2; Ov. sup., 2-celled, stigma 2-lobed. Fr. a 2-parted capsule, each half a 1/4" globe. March - May.

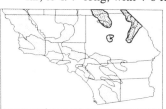

Desert ashes *(Fraxinus)*

Olive Family (Oleaceae)

Key to species:

1 **A**—Leaves typically simple (rarely 2- or 3-foliate), roundish, hairless on both surfaces, 3/4 - 2" long; young twigs 4-sided; wings of nut extend almost to base . . . . **Singleleaf ash** *(F. anomala)*

B—Leaves pinnately compound, 4-6" long, with 3-7 leaflets, hairless above, velvety-hairy below when young; young twigs rounded; wings of fruit barely reach middle of nut . . . . **Velvet ash** *(F. velutina)*

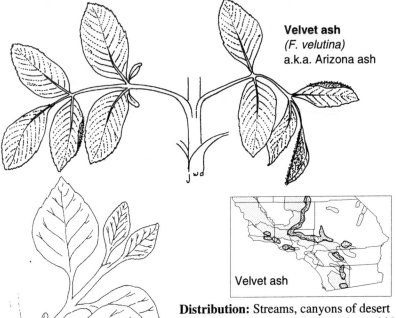

Velvet ash
(F. velutina)
a.k.a. Arizona ash

Velvet ash

Singleleaf ash
(F. anomala)
a.k.a. Dwarf ash

Distribution: Streams, canyons of desert mountains, below 5000' (Velvet), 3000-11000' (Singleleaf); Cha, SOW, YPF (Velvet), PJW (Singleleaf).

Description: Small, deciduous, trees or tree-like shrubs, to 20' (singleleaf) or 30' (velvet). Lvs. opp. Flrs. small, in many-flowered clusters (panicles), appearing before or with first leaves. Ca. with 4 small teeth; Pe. none; St. 2 (rarely 3 or 4). Fr. a flattened, winged, nut-like samara. Mar. - June.

Related species: California ash *(F. dipetala)* occurs in the coastal foothills throughout most of so. California.

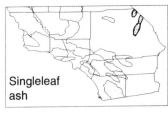

Singleleaf ash

Fremont cottonwood *(Populus fremontii)*

a.k.a White or Alamo cottonwood   Willow Family (Salicaceae)

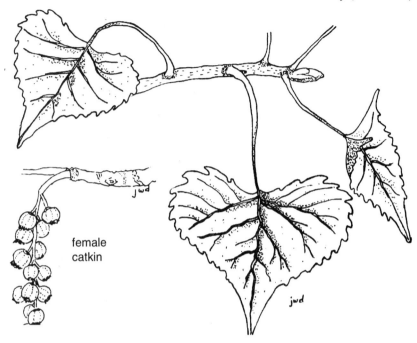

female catkin

Distribution: Streams, moist places, below 6000' in Mojave Desert, and western edge of Colorado Desert; RiW.

Description: Handsome, broad-leaved tree with open crown, to 90' tall. Lvs. alt., deciduous, light yellow-green above, slightly lighter below, blade somewhat wider (2 1/2 - 3") than long (2 - 2 1/2"), broadly heartshaped or flat at base, tapering to a point, edges irregularly tooth, the 1 1/2- 3" long petiole flattened. Flrs. in catkins, sepals and petals lacking: male catkins 1 1/2 - 2" long with 60+ red stamens; female catkins shorter, sparsely flowered, ovary 1-celled, stigmas 3. Fr. a 3-valved capsule. Seeds white hairy. Feb. - April.

Notes: The cottony seeds that waft in the breeze and cover the ground at fruiting time provide these plants their appropriate vernacular names. Fremont cottonwood is a "true cottonwood," its leaves broader than long, their stalks flattened so that they flutter in the breeze as do those of Quaking aspen. Mojave Indians used the bark to make skirts.

Related species: A variety of Fremont cottonwood with bluish-green leaves and densely hairy young shoots and petioles is found among the ditches and streams feeding the Colorado River. This form of the plant is considered by some botanists to be a species in its own right (*P. macdougallii*).

Willows *(Salix)*

Key to species (Only common desert forms are included, but others occur):

1 | A—A tree or large shrub, to 30' tall; male flowers with 4-5 stamens; leaf
blades hairless below (except when young); petioles distinct, up to 3/8"
long; catkins attached by a leafy branchlet up to 1 3/4" long; plant of
Colorado River drainage, below 2000' . . . .
. . . . **Goodding's willow** *(S. gooddingii)*
B—A shrub, rarely taller than 12'; male flowers with 2 stamens; leaf blades
usually hairy below (occasionally hairless in Arroyo willow); petioles
commonly reaching 1/2" or lacking altogether; catkins either attached
directly to stem or by a stalk up to 3" long . . . . Go to 2

2 | A—Leaves narrow (less than 3/8"), without a distinct petiole; blades hairy
on both surfaces; leaf edges finely sawtoothed; catkins attached to a
leafy stalk up to 3" long; common throughout both deserts and on
adjoining mountains to 8000' . . . . **Narrow-leaved willow** *(S. exigua)*
B—Leaves lance-shaped, mostly 3/8 - 1" wide, the petiole commonly reaching 1/2"; blades hairless above, either hairless or hairy below; leaf edges
smooth, somewhat rolled under; catkins attach directly to stem; plant
occasional in deserts, primarily along western edges to 7000' . . . .
. . . . **Arroyo willow** *(S. lasiolepis)*

Distribution: Wet places, streams, ditches, ponds. Goodding's; CBS, CSS.
Narrow-leaved; SBS, CBS, PJW, YPF. Arroyo; many plant communities.

Description: Deciduous shrubs or trees. Lvs. simple, alt., at least 4 times
longer than wide, often with deciduous stipules at base. Flrs. in catkins,
male and female catkins on separate plants; scale-like bract at base of each
flr. Se. and Pe. lacking; St. 2 or more; Ov. 1-celled. Fr. 2-valved capsule
with many small seeds each tufted with fine hairs. Spring-early summer.

Notes: Willows are stream-, lake- and pond-side inhabitants. Their general
form is familiar to just about everyone. Mule Fat *(Baccharis salicifolia)*
and Desert willow *(Chilopsis linearis)* are commonly confused with true
willows. Mule Fat, a member of the Sunflower family, is readily identified
by its globose composite flower heads; Desert willow's leaves are exceeding long and narrow, its large flower conspicuous when in bloom.

The inner bark of willow stems may be eaten in an emergency. The dried
wood of the stems make excellent drills for initiating fires using the old
technique of rapidly twirling a stick against a flattened base.

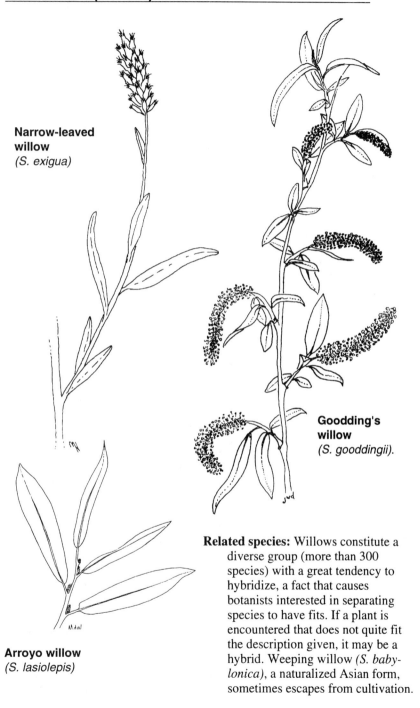

Narrow-leaved willow
(S. exigua)

Goodding's willow
(S. gooddingii).

Arroyo willow
(S. lasiolepis)

Related species: Willows constitute a diverse group (more than 300 species) with a great tendency to hybridize, a fact that causes botanists interested in separating species to have fits. If a plant is encountered that does not quite fit the description given, it may be a hybrid. Weeping willow *(S. babylonica)*, a naturalized Asian form, sometimes escapes from cultivation.

Desert oaks *(Quercus)*

Beech Family (Fagaceae)

Key to species:

1 A—Lower leaf surface whitish, densely covered with fine hair that obscures lateral veins; upper leaf surface yellow- or gray-green; leaf edge smooth, or with round-tipped lobe; plant of granite slopes of San Bernardino, Little San Bernardino Mtns. . . . . **Muller's oak** *(Q. cornelius-mulleri)*

   B—Lower leaf surface greenish, hairs not obscuring lateral veins; upper surface dull, gray-green; leaf edge lobed, the lobes sharp-pointed . Go to 2

2 A—Acorn yellow-brown, not exceeding 1"long, attached by stalk up to 1/2" long; lower leaf surface with yellow star-shaped or glandular hairs; plant of the eastern Mojave Desert mountains (New York Mtns.), 3800-6200' . . . . **Scrub live oak** *(Q. turbinella)*

   B—Acorn dark brown, to 1 1/4" long, stalkless, attached directly to stem; lower leaf surface pale gray-green, fine haired; plant of desert-facing slope of San Gabriel Mtns., 2800-6200' . **Tucker's oak** *(Q. john-tuckeri)*

Distribution: Desert mtn. slopes; Cha, PJW (Tucker's, Muller's), PJW (Scrub).

Scrub live oak *(Q. turbinella)*

Description: Shrubby oaks, rarely tree-like. Lvs. alt. Male flrs. in slim, drooping catkins clustered in leaf axils: Ca. minute, 4- to 6 - lobed; St. 2-6. Female flrs. solitary or in few-flowered. spikes: Ca. 6-lobed, fused to ovary; Ov. inf., 3-celled, styles 3. Calyx enclosed by a cup of overlapping scales that becomes acorn cap. March - May.

Notes: The acorns of most oaks were a staple food for Indians, but those of these and other scrub oaks were generally ignored. Many animals, such as mountain sheep, depend on the acorns for food. The oaks are a large and confusing group, but these are the only ones likely to be found in the deserts, mainly on the fringes.

White alder *(Alnus rhombifolia)*
a.k..a. Western alder, Calif. alder   Birch Family (Betulaceae)

Distribution: Along streams on western fringes of both deserts; RiW.

Description: A tree, 30-100' tall, with a straight, gray-brown, trunk and spreading branches. Lvs. oval, apex rounded or slightly pointed, 2-4" long, 1 1/2 - 2" across (larger on new shoots); blade dark green, mostly hairless above, yellow-green and minutely downy beneath, edges finely and irregularly toothed (sometimes doubly so). Flrs. in catkins. Male catkins 1-6" long, pendulous, 2 to several in a cluster; Ca. 3- to 5-parted; St. 3 to 5. Female catkins 1/2 - 3/4" long, woody and cone-like at maturity. Jan.- April.

White alder (con't)

Notes: This graceful tree is not truly a member of our desert flora, occurring only on the deserts' western-most fringes where streams flowing from our mountains provide suitable conditions. The only member of the birch family that attains tree size in southern California, this tree is much more typical of the coastal region where it is commonly seen along streams.

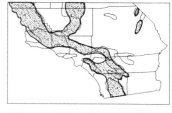

Though the female catkins of this tree resemble small cones, White alder is a flowering plant, not a conifer. The tree is widely cultivated for its shade. Indians made dye for their baskets and a tonic to encourage sweating in their "sweat houses" from the plant

Silk tassel bush *(Garrya flavescens)*

a.k.a. Quinine bush   Silk tassel family (Garryaceae)

Distribution: Desert slopes; Cha, PJW.

Description: Erect, 4-8' tall shrub with densely white-woolly young twigs. Lvs. opp., simple, leathery, elliptical, 1- 3" long, 3/4 - 1 3/4" wide, hairless above, often densely wavy haired below, the leaf edges smooth, either flat or undulating. Flrs. small, without petals, in 2 - 4" long pendulous catkins, 2 -4 catkins per cluster. Male flrs. in groups of 6 - 10: Se. 4; St. 4. Female flrs. in pairs in bract axils: Ca. 2-lobed; ov. inf., 1-celled, 2-styled. Fr. a densely hairy, drupe-like berry.

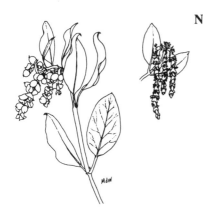

Notes: There are several species of silk tassel bushes in southern California. Most are associated with the chaparral region, but some occasionally occur along the margins of deserts. Only this species, however, occurs in the desert proper, mainly in the desert mountains. This and other silk tassel bushes make handsome ornamental shrubs, their long catkins adding a distinctive character. The leaves contain a bitter alkaloid that gives the plants their alternate name, Quinine bush.

Ephedra or Desert tea *(Ephedra)*

a.k.a. Indian tea, Squaw tea, Mexican tea   Ephedra Family (Ephedraceae)
Mormon tea, Miner's tea, Joint fir

Key to species:

1   **A**—Scale-like leaves occur in pairs; cones attached by a basal stalk and with 2 bracts beneath them . . . . Go to 2
    B—Scale-like leaves in threes (rarely in pairs); cones without a basal stalk and having 3 bracts beneath them . . . . Go to 5

2   **A**—Branches rough to the touch; bases of leaves brown . . . . Go to 3
    B—Branches smooth to the touch; bases of leaves gray . . . . Go to 4

3   **A**—Branches bright green or yellowish-green; seeds dark brown or black, in pairs; plant common between 3000' and 7500' in foothills of Mojave Desert or on w. edge of Colorado Desert . . **Green ephedra** (*E. viridis*)
    B—Branches dark green to greenish-yellow; seeds rusty-brown, occurring singly; plant occasional below 5000' in either desert . . . . . *E. aspera*

4   **A**—Branches gray or brownish green; seeds smooth, dark brown or black, in pairs; plant common in both deserts below 4500'. . . . .
    . . . . **Nevada ephedra** (*E. nevadensis*)
    B—Branches green to yellow; seeds rough, light brown to gray-green, occurring singly; plant occasional in sandy places . . . . *E. fasciculata*

5   **A**—Branches blunt-tipped, yellow-green, smooth except for longitudinal furrows; plant common below 3000' in both deserts . . . .
    . . . . **Desert tea** (*E. californica*)
    B—Branches spine-tipped, light green to gray- or yellowish-green, almost smooth; plant rare, found only below 2000' in Imperial Co. or near Daggett in the Mojave Desert . . . . *E. trifurca*

Distribution: All species are found in Creosote Bush Scrub; those that occur in the Mojave Desert also inhabit Joshua Tree Woodlands. Green ephedra is common in the Pinyon-juniper Woodlands as well, and Desert tea reaches the Chaparral in San Diego Co. where its range extends to the coast.

Description: All are erect, apparently leafless, broom-like shrubs with jointed, branches; rarely more than 4' tall, usually much less. Triangular, scale-like leaves appear at the joints. Reproduction by means of soft cones (strobili) rather than flowers; cones borne in the axils of the branches, the male and female cones occurring on separate plants.

Ephedra or Desert tea (con't)

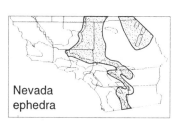

Nevada
ephedra

Notes: As the vernacular names imply, these plants were used by native Americans and early settlers to produce a tea that served both as a tonic and as a beverage. The tea, brewed from the dried stems, contains an ephedrine-like chemical, hence provides a "lift" not unlike that obtained from coffee and other caffeine-containing drinks. The medicinal drug ephedrin, a mild stimulant used in the treatment of colds, asthma and hay fever, is obtained from a related Asian species, *E. sinica*. Native Americans roasted the seeds, eating them whole or grinding them into a flour; they considered the tea a treatment for venereal diseases. All species are apparently browsed by bighorn sheep and deer, especially in winter when other forage is scarce.

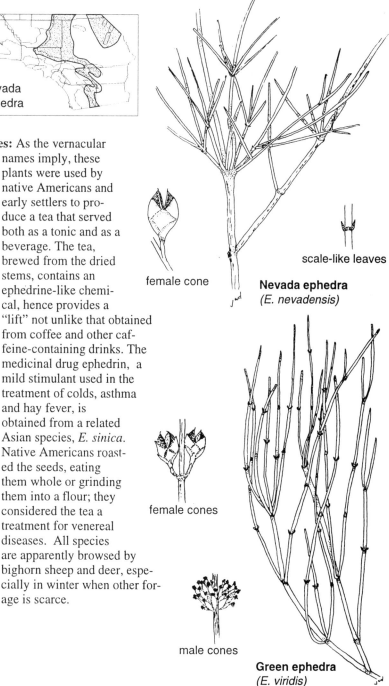

female cone

scale-like leaves

Nevada ephedra
(E. nevadensis)

female cones

male cones

Green ephedra
(E. viridis)

Junipers *(Juniperus)*

Cypress Family (Cupressaceae)

Key to species:

1 **A**—A tree, to 50' tall, with red-brown bark; mature cones ("berries") blue-black; leaves in 3's around stem, producing 6 rows of leaves; plant of desert slopes of San Gabriel, San Bernardino Mtns. or of mountains of Mojave Desert, to 9000' . **Sierra juniper** *(J. occidentalis* var. *australis)*

   B—A shrub (sometimes a small tree, to 25') with gray to gray-brown bark; cones red-brown when mature; leaves in pairs or 3's . . . . Go to 2

2 **A**—Leaves in 3s around stem, hence in 6 rows; distinct resin pit on back of each leaf; male and female cones on separate plants, female cones 3/8 - 5/8" long; many secondary trunks arising near ground; plant grows below 5000' on slopes on western edge of both deserts and in the mountains of Mojave Desert . . . .**California juniper** *(J. californica)*

   B—Leaves in pairs (rarely 3s), making four rows along stem; resin pit on leaves missing or obscure; male and female cones on same plant, female cones 3/16 - 3/8" long; usually with a short trunk; plant of the mountains of the eastern Mojave Desert or of desert slopes of San Bernardino or San Gabriel Mtns., above 4000' . . . . . **Utah juniper** *(J. osteosperma)*

Distribution: Mostly in association with pinyons or Joshua tree; PJW, JTW (all), Cha (Calif.), YPF (Sierra).

Description: Aromatic shrubs or trees. Lvs. scale-like, appressed to and completely covering branchlets; leaf tips sharp pointed and flaring on young shoots. Male cones minute, alone or in clusters, 3-6 pollen sacs per scale. Female cones with 3-8 fleshy scales that fuse into a roundish "berry." Jan. - March, fruits maturing second season.

California juniper
(J. californica)

Notes: California juniper, with fruits that persist through the lean winter months, served Indians well as a survival food. Its astringent berries were sometimes eaten raw but more commonly were dried and later cooked in a stew or ground into a meal for inclusion in cakes or mush. The berries were also used to make a tea to treat fevers or colds, as was a concoction brewed from the bark. The shreddy bark served as mattress stuffing and as a source of red dye. Juniper berries are used commercially to give flavor to gin and their oil has been used widely in patent medicines.

Calif. juniper

Pinyon pines *(Pinus)*

Pine Family (Pinaceae)

Key to species:

1 |**A**—Needles occur singly and are round in cross section; tree grows from 2000 to 5000' (or occasionally to 9000') in foothills of our desert mountains . . . . **Singleleaf pinyon pine** *(P. monophylla)*
  B—Needles occur in bundles of 2 or 4 and are not round . . . . . . Go to 2

2 |**A**—Needles 2 to a bundle, deeply channeled; tree grows in New York or Little San Bernardino Mtns., 4500 - 7000' . . . .
  . . . . **Colorado pinyon pine** *(P. edulis)*
  B—Needles 4 per bundle, pale green above, whitish below; tree grows from 3500 to 5500' on Colorado Desert's western edge . . . .
  . . . . **Parry pinyon pine** *(P. quadrifolia)*

Description: Short-trunked, scraggly trees, rarely exceeding 40' tall. Lvs. 1 1/2 to 2" needles. Seed cones small with large, nut-like seeds.

Notes: The large seeds of the pinyon pines were favored food of the southwestern Indians. Pinyon seeds are nutritious, rich in both protein and fat; with 3000 calories per pound they are also a substantial source of energy. Green cones were roasted to remove the pitch and cause them to open, after which the seeds were easily removed. Shelled, the seeds were eaten fresh or parched and pounded into a flour used to make cakes. The gum of the tree was used to waterproof baskets, served as glue in pot repair, and was chewed to ease sore throats. Colorado pinyon pine, considered rare and endangered, occurs in southern California only in two localities, but is common in the neighboring states of Arizona, Nevada and Utah.

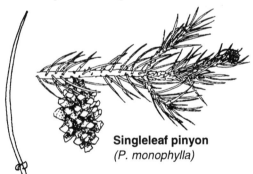

Singleleaf pinyon
(P. monophylla)

Parry pinyon pine
(P. quadrifolia)
a.k.a. Four-leaved pinyon

Colorado pinyon pine
(P. edulis)
a.k.a. Common pinyon

Desert chollas *(Opuntia)*

Cactus Family (Cactaceae)

Key to species:

1 A—Branches slightly larger in diameter than a pencil (less than 3/8"); spines solitary . . . . **Pencil cholla** *(O. ramosissima)*
    B—Branches thicker, 3/4" or more across; spines in clusters . . . . Go to 2

2 A—Branches densely covered with straw-colored spines arising in groups of 6-8; branches tightly clustered at the top of a dark brown or black trunk that itself often contributes about half the height of the plant . . . . . .
    . . . . **Teddy-bear cholla** *(O. bigelovii)*
    B—Branches loosely covered with spines arising in groups of 10 or more; branches not tightly clustered and trunk, if present, not black . . Go to 3

3 A—Terminal branch segments less than 6" long; trunk present but rarely exceeding 1/3 the plant's height; crown broad, dense . . . .
    . . . . **Silver cholla** *(O. echinocarpa)*
    B—Terminal branch segments commonly exceed 6"; trunk lacking or contributing less than 1/5 the plant's height; crown open . . . .
    . . . . **Buckhorn cholla** *(O. acanthocarpa)*

Distribution: Dry washes, alluvial fans, slopes, mesas in both deserts. Teddy-bear cholla rarely grows above 3000', pencil and buckhorn cholla reach 4500, silver cholla 6000'; CBS, JTW (all), PJW (silver cholla).

Description: Leafless, succulent-stemmed shrubs, with spines encased in a loose, papery sheath. Flrs. solitary, large, yellowish-green streaked with red (Pencil, Silver), pale green to lavender (Teddy-bear), or red, yellow or greenish-yellow (Buckhorn). Se. thick, green or partly colored, intergrading with petals; Pe. many, longer than sepals; St. many, shorter than petals. Fr. a many-seeded berry, spineless and fleshy (Teddy-bear) or spiny and dry (others) at maturity. April - June.

Notes: All chollas, covered as they are with spines, are potential dangers to the unwary. Teddy-bear cholla has earned (rightfully!) a reputation as the most formidable. Not only do its long, thin spines readily penetrate flesh or clothing, microscopic barbs near a spine's apex virtually assure that they remain imbedded. Moreover, the branch segments detach readily from the plant so that contact with one spine usually means the entire segment follows; it is from this that its alternate name, Jumping cholla, derives, for it does seem as though the plant literally jumps at those who venture too close. In addition, the branches are commonly found lying on the ground just waiting to snag a shoe or pant leg. Most seeds of jumping cholla are incapable of germinating, hence the species depends for its perpetuation upon the rooting of these fallen branches, dispersed by humans and animals to which they attach. Wood rats commonly collect great mounds of cholla branches around their nests, providing a nearly impenetrable fortress for themselves and their young. Surprisingly, these animals seem to enter and leave their nests across the thicket of spines with no difficulty.

Desert chollas (con't)

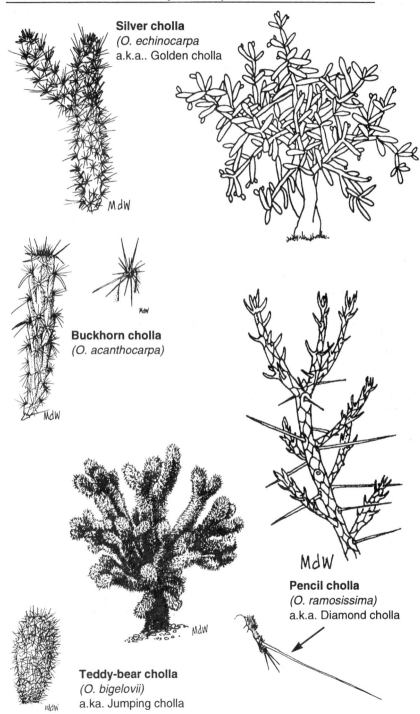

Silver cholla
(O. echinocarpa
a.k.a.. Golden cholla

MdW

Buckhorn cholla
(O. acanthocarpa)

MdW

Teddy-bear cholla
(O. bigelovii)
a.ka. Jumping cholla

Pencil cholla
(O. ramosissima)
a.k.a. Diamond cholla

MdW

Desert prickly pears *(Opuntia)*

Cactus Family (Cactaceae)

Key to species:

1 **A**—Plant almost tree-like, up to 10' tall, with a stout, distinctive trunk; spines yellow, mostly pointing downward, becoming dense on older stem sections to produce a hairy look; uncommon in mountains of the Mojave Desert, 2000-3800' . . . . **Pancake prickly pear** *(O. chlorotica)*
  B—Plant not tree-like, lacking distinct trunk; spines not as above   . Go to 2

2 **A**—Plant scarcely 1' tall; branch segments elongate, less than 3" across; spines commonly 5" or more long, white to pale gray; plant of San Jacinto Mtn. and Mojave Desert, especially its mountains (including San Bernardino Mtn, 2500-8000'. . . **Old man prickly pear** *(O. erinacea)*
  B—Plant taller; branch segments nearly round, wider; spines rarely exceeding 3" in length, red-brown at base . . . . Go to 3

3 **A**—Stem sections typically greater than 6" across; up to 12 spines per cluster; inner flesh of fruit red; flowers yellow at base; uncommon in San Jacinto Mtns. and in mountains of Mojave Desert, 3000-5000' . . . . . .
  . . . . **Engelmann prickly pear** *(O. engelmannii)*
  B—Stem sections typically less than 6" across; rarely more than 4 spines per cluster; inner flesh of fruit green; flowers red at base; plant widespread in both deserts, to 7000' . . . . . . **Mojave prickly pear** *(O. phaeacantha)*

Distribution: Dry, rocky slopes and canyon walls; CBS, JTW, PJW.

Description: The branch segments of all prickly pears are flattened and spine-covered. Flrs. solitary, large. Se. thick, green or partly colored, intergrading with petals; Pe. many, longer than sepals; St. many, much shorter than petals. Fr. dry and short-spined (Old man prickly pear) or fleshy, purplish and spineless others). May - June.

Notes: The fleshy pulp of prickly pear fruits is edible either raw or cooked into a jam.

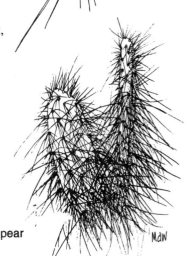

Old man prickly pear
(O. erinacea)

MdW

136

Desert prickly pears (con't)

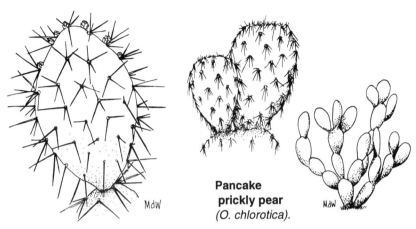

Pancake prickly pear
(O. chlorotica).

Mojave prickly pear
(O. phaeacantha)

Beavertail cactus *(Opuntia basilaris)*
Cactus Family (Cactaceae)

Distribution: Dry, sandy washes and arid slopes of both deserts to 4000'; CBS, JTW. Also UT, NV, AZ, no. Mex.

Description: Low, spreading plants, usually in clumps, seldom taller than 12". Stems blue-green to purplish, flattened, branching mostly from base. Branch segments 3-6" long, 2-5" wide, lacking spines, but with many small areoles each bearing a cluster of tiny, barbed bristles (glochid hairs). Flrs. large, showy, deep rose to purple, clustered at upper edge of branch segments. Se. thick, green or partly colored, intergrading with petals; Pe. many, longer than sepals; St. many, shorter than petals. Fr. a dry, brown or grey spine- less berry at maturity. March-June.

Notes: S.W. Indians found many uses for this plant. After carefully rubbing them in sand to remove the glochids, the young fruit were pit-roasted and eaten. The fleshy stems were cut into strips and added to other food or were dried (after burning off the glochids) in the sun and stored, sometimes for years, until needed; boiling and a little salt made them palatable. The pulp was used as a dressing for injuries and is said to deaden pain. Warts were removed by rubbing glochids into them.

137

Saguaro *(Carnegiea gigantea)*

a.k.a. Sahuaro, Giant cactus   Cactus Family (Cactaceae)

Distribution: Found in Calif. in only in a few locations on well-drained soil near the Colorado River, below 1500'; CBS. Common in Arizona, northern Mexico.

Description: A tall (to 50'), columnar cactus, with a few simple, up-turned branches high above the base when mature. Trunk to 12' thick, with 12-24 prominent ribs converging at apex. Spines on ribs, in clusters of 10-25 with tufts of brown felt; central spine often 2" or more long. Flrs. white, below tips of branches, opening at night. Fr. green, red within, sparsely spiny, fleshy when mature, 2-3" long. May-June.

Notes: No other plant symbolizes the southwestern deserts as does the saguaro. Its unique form is immortalized in numerous paintings and photographs and is known the world over from postcards. It is in Arizona, however, that the plant grows most luxuriously, often in dense stands. Plant is long-lived, occasionally achieving 150-200 years. Branching begins about age 75.

Arizona Indians ate the fruit fresh or in a preserve. The fruit's juice was fermented to produce an intoxicating drink. Seeds were sometimes ground into a sort of mealy butter.

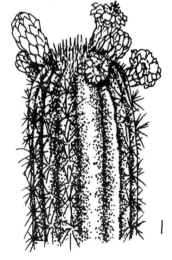

Calif. barrel cactus (*Ferocactus cylindraceus*)

Cactus Family (Cactaceae)

Distribution: Gravelly soils, rocky walls and slopes of canyons below 5000' in Colorado and eastern Mojave Deserts; CBS, JTW. Also NV, UT, AZ, no. Mex.

Description: An erect, unbranched, barrel-like, ribbed cactus typically 3-6' tall, 12-16" wide at maturity. Ribs vertical, to 1" high, 20-30 in number. Spines yellow to red or brown, in clusters; central spines of cluster 2-6" long, flattened, spreading, often twisted and hooked at end, marked with lines or rings; peripheral spines shorter, stouter, less curved. Flrs. funnel-shaped, yellow, borne at apex of plant. Fr. fleshy, yellow to greenish, spineless, to 1 1/4" long. April - May.

Notes: In times of emergency, s.w. Indians pounded the pulp to release its moisture. Spines were used as awls or needles and buds were roasted and eaten. Some tribes used the cactus as a sort of oven; after removing the pulp from the center, the chamber was heated with hot rocks.

MdW

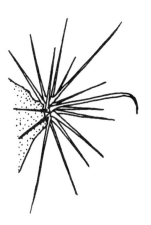

Glossary of specialized terms

achene. A dry, hard, one-seeded fruit that does not split open.

acorn. A nut, the base of which is enclosed by a woody cup; the fruit of an oak.

alternate. An arrangement of leaves or leaflets along a stem or rachis such that they occur first on one side, then the other; an arrangement of flower parts such that they regularly occur between rather than in line with another flower part.

anther. An enlarged, saclike structure at the tip of a stamen that bears the pollen.

apetalous. Without petals.

appressed. Closely pressed against another structure, as scalelike leaves appressed to the stem.

areole. An area from which spines or flowers arise in cacti.

armed. Bearing spines or prickles.

aromatic. Producing a strong scent or odor.

axil. The angle between a leaf and the stem from which it arises.

axillary. Arising from an axil.

banner. The rearmost, large, upright petal of a papilionaceous (pea) flower.

berry. Fruit developing from a compound ovary that is fleshy throughout and lacks a true stone, e.g. tomato, orange or strawberry.

bipinnate. Twice pinnate, that is, the leaflets themselves divided into still smaller leaflets.

blade. Flattened or expanded portion of a leaf.

bloom. A powdery or waxy coating on a fruit or leaf that readily rubs off.

bract. A small, modified leaf arising in association with a flower or an inflorescence; a narrow structure at the base of the scales of a cone.

bractlet. A small bract.

bur. A fruit with hooks or prickles on its surface.

burl. A woody swelling where the stems join the roots.

calyx. All of the sepals together; the outermost whorl of parts in a flower.

capsule. A dry fruit that splits into two or more pieces on ripening.

carpel. A simple pistil or one of the parts of a compound pistil.

catkin. A slender, usually dangling, cluster of unisexual flowers.

cell. A chamber of an ovary in which ovules develop.

chaparral. A plant community dominated by drought-resistant, thick-leaved shrubs; see page 16-18.

clasping. Said of a leaf whose base partially or wholly surrounds the stem.

coastal sage scrub. A shrub-dominated plant community near the coast of southern California; see page 16-18.

coastal salt marsh. The plant assemblage that occurs in the coastal inlets and estuaries frequently inundated by sea water; see page 16-18.

coastal strand. An assemblage of low shrubs and herbs occupying the sandy dunes and slopes near the coast of southern California; see page 16-18.

composite head. A cluster of small, tubular flowers underlain by an involucre, e.g. daisy or sunflower.

compound leaf. A leaf composed of two or more leaflike parts or leaflets.

compound. Composed on two or more similar parts.

cone. A reproductive structure composed of scales arranged around an axis, each scale bearing either anthers (male cones) or ovules that become seeds (female cones); often woody, as in pines, but may be fleshy, as in junipers.

coniferous. Cone-bearing.

corolla. All of the petals together; the whorl of flower parts just within the calyx.

cyme. A flat-topped inflorescence with flowers arising alternately along the stem and in which the central flowers are the first to open.

deciduous. Falling at maturity or with a change in the seasons.

dichotomous. Branching regularly and repeatedly in pairs.

dioecious. Having male and female flowers borne on different plants (see monoecious).

disc flower. A tubular flower that occurs in the central portion of a composite head.

disc. All the tubular (discoid) flowers together in the center of a compound head; a fleshy growth from the receptacle that wholly or partially surrounds the base of an ovary.

discoid head. A head composed of disc flowers only, the ray flowers completely lacking.

discoid. Of or associated with the disc of a composite head.

distinct. Separate; not united.

drupe. A fruit composed of a single seed, or stone, surrounded by a fleshy pulp.

evergreen. Retaining its leaves all years; not deciduous.

family. A taxonomic grouping composed of related genera.

fascicle. A tight cluster of leaves, flowers or other parts arising together from a common point.

fertile. Capable of reproduction; said of a stamen that bears an anther or a carpel that bears ovules.

filament. The stalk of a stamen.

fruit. A ripened ovary and all its accessory parts.

genus. A taxonomic grouping including from one to several closely related species.

gland. A structure, either embedded in the surface or at the end of a protuberance, that secretes a usually sticky substance.

glochid. A barbed hair or bristle.

head. See *composite head*.

hemispheric. In the shape of half a sphere.

herb. A non-woody plant.

herbaceous. Composed of non-woody parts.

hypanthium. A cup-shaped outgrowth of the receptacle of some flowers to which the calyx, corolla and sometimes stamens are attached.

inferior. Said of an ovary that is situated below the point of attachment of the calyx.

inflorescence. A cluster of flowers; an arrangement of flowers on the stem.

internode. The length of stem between two adjacent nodes.

involucral bract. One of a series of leaflike structures that underlie and surround the base of a composite head; a phyllary.

involucre. A whorl of bracts (phyllaries) that underlies a cluster of flowers, especially those that make up a composite head.

irregular. Not radially symmetrical; said of a flower in which the flower parts in a given whorl (petals, sepals, etc.) are dissimilar.

joint. The point of articulation of two parts; a section of a stem of a cactus.

keel. A prominent ridge reminiscent of the keel of a boat; the two partially fused petals of a papilionaceous flower that inclose the reproductive parts.

keeled. Having or bearing a keel.

leaflet. A leaflike division of a compound leaf; a pinna.

legume. A fruit (pod) from a one-celled pistil that splits when mature along two lines into two halves;a plant that bears such a fruit.

ligule. A tonguelike structure extending from one side of the corolla of a ray flower; a ray.

lip. One of the two divisions of a two-lipped corolla or calyx.

lobe. Any division of an organ, as, for instance, of a leaf, calyx or corolla.

monoecious. Having male and female reproductive parts in different flowers on the same plant (see dioecious).

needle. A stiff, linear leaf, usually of a coniferous plant.

node. The point of attachment of a leaf to the stem.

nut. A dry, one-seeded, hard-shelled fruit from a compound ovary that does not split open at maturity.

opposite. Set against one another, as when leaves arise in opposing pairs along a stem, or a stamen arises immediately adjacent to a petal.

ovary. The basal, usually swollen portion of the pistil in which the ovule form.

ovule. A reproductive structure that, upon being fertilized, becomes a seed.

palmate. Having veins or leaflets radiating outward from a common point, like the fingers from the palm of the hand.

panicle. An compound raceme.

papilionaceous. Of or pertaining to the flower of the pea, the petals composed of three types: banner, wings, and keel.

pedicel. The stalk of a single flower within a flower cluster.

perfect. Having male and female reproductive parts (stamens and pistils) in the same flower.

perianth. Sepals and petals together; typically used when sepals and petals are similar in form and not easily distinguished.

petal. One member of the whorl of flower parts, usually brightly colored and showy, that lie just within the calyx and surrounding the reproductive parts.

petiole. The stalklike base of a leaf or leaflet.

phyllary. One of a series of leaflike structures that underlie and surround the base of a composite head; an involucral bract.

pinna. One of the primary divisions of a compound leaf; a leaflet.

pinnate. Arranged like a feather with veins or leaflets arising on either side of a midrib or rachis.

pistil. A female reproductive part of a flower, consisting of an ovary, style and stigma.

pistillate. Bearing pistils, i.e. female; said of flowers with pistils but lacking stamens.

pod. Any dry fruit that opens at maturity along sutures; a legume.

pollen. The male reproductive cells produced in the anther.

pome. A fleshy fruit developing from a compound ovary in which the receptacle is included in the fruit, as in an apple.

prickle. A sharp, usually small, spine or thorn.

raceme. An inflorescence in which the flowers are borne on stalks (pedicels) arising along a single stem or rachis.

rachis. The central axis of a pinnately-compound leaf or of an inflorescence.

ray flower. An irregular flower, usually arranged around the margin of a composite head, in which the corolla is elongated on one side to form a petallike structure (ligule or ray).

ray. A tonguelike structure that extends from one side of the corolla of a ray flower; a ligule.

receptacle. The enlarged tip of a floral axis that bears a flower or, in the sunflower family, a flower head.

regular. Radially symmetrical; said of a flower in which the flower parts in a given whorl (petals, sepals, etc.) are similar.

riparian woodland. A plant assemblage found naturally along watercourses; see page 16-18.

rosette. A cluster of leaves arising together from the ground.

scale. A small, vestigial leaf, usually without a petiole and often closely appressed to the stem.

seed. A mature, fertilized ovule.

sepal . A member of the outermost whorl of flower parts (calyx) that encloses the flower when in bud.

sessile. Attached directly without a basal stalk.

shrub. A woody plant with several branches arising from the base, hence without a distinctive trunk.

simple. Not branched; composed of a single part.

solitary. Occurring alone, as in a single flower borne at the end of a flower stalk.

southern oak woodland. A plant community dominated by oak trees, usually found in sheltered canyons; see page 16-18.

species. A group of organisms, all members of which are similar in form and capable of mating with each other and producing fertile offspring.

spike. An elongate inflorescence in which the flowers are attached directly (i.e. without a pedicel) to a single rachis.

spine. Any stiff, sharp-pointed, usually woody, structure; a thorn.

spinose. Bearing spines.

stamen. The male (pollen-bearing) reproductive structure, typically consisting of an anther and its supporting filament.

staminate. Bearing stamens, i.e. male; said of flowers with stamens but lacking pistils.

stellate. Starlike, with branches radiating outward in all directions from the center.

sterile. Incapable of reproducing; said of a stamen that lacks an anther or a carpel that lacks ovules.

stigma. The part of the pistil, usually at the tip, that receives the pollen.

stipule. One of a pair of leaflike structures attached at the base of a leaf in some plants.

stoma. Small apertures in a leaf surface through which air passes.

stomata. The plural of stoma.

stone. A hard, seed-enclosing structure within a drupe.

strobilus. A cone, woody or not.

style. The outgrowth of an ovary that supports the stigma.

succulent. Fleshy, soft, swollen with water; said of the branches of cacti and the leaves of many plants.

superior. Said of an ovary that is situated entirely above the point of attachment of the calyx.

thorn. Any sharp-pointed woody structure; a spine.

throat. The expanded portion of a tubular or funnel-shaped corolla just within the mouth.

toothed. Composed of sharp, toothlike projections or lobes.

tree. A woody plant having a single main trunk from which the other branches arise.

trifoliate. Having three leaflets.

tube. The narrow part of a corolla composed of fused petals.

tubercle. A raised, wartlike structure.

two-lipped. Divided into an upper and a lower part, as at the mouth of the corolla (or calyx) of many flowers with united petals (or sepals).

umbel. A flat-topped inflorescence in which all the flowers arise from a common point on the stem.

unarmed. Without spines or prickles.

valley grassland. A treeless, grass-dominated plant community that was formerly common in the valleys of southern California; see page 16-18.

vein. A strand of vascular tissue passing through a leaf.

venation. An arrangement of veins.

whorl. Three or more similar organs (leaves, petals, sepals, etc.) arising in a circle around an axis.

wing. One of two lateral petals in a papilionaceous flower; any wing-like structure.

woolly. Covered with long, soft hairs.

Abbreviations used

Plant communities *		Other	
AlS	= Alkali Sink	"	= inches
CBS	= Creosote Bush Scrub	'	= feet
Cha.	= Chaparral	Alt.	= alternate
CoS	= Coastal Strand	Ca.	= calyx
CSM	= Coastal Salt Marsh	Co.	= corolla; county
CSS	= Coastal Sage Scrub	Flr.	= flower
FhW	= Foothill Woodland	Fr.	= fruit
JTW	= Joshua Tree Woodland	Lflts.	= leaflets
PJW	= Pinyon-Juniper Woodland	Lvs.	= leaves
RiW	= Riparian Woodland	Opp.	= opposite
SbS	= Sagebrush Scrub	Ov.	= ovary
SOW	= Southern Oak Woodland	Pe.	= petal
SsS	= Shadscale Scrub	Pi.	= pistil
VGr	= Valley Grassland	Se.	= sepal
YPF	= Yellow Pine Forest	St.	= stamen
		Sup.	= superior

* for additional information about
plant communities, see pages 16-18.

Index

C

EXOTICS   Melia azedarach

Chinaberry - large tree neighbors behind Hacienda.
Blooming all over. pretty lav. flowers
Leat   Mahogony Family / Asia

See p. 183 Plants E. Mojave